TAKE YOUR BABY AND RUN

How nurses blew the whistle on Canada's biggest cardiac disaster

Carol Youngson

GREAT PLAINS
PRESS

Great Plains Press
320 Rosedale Ave
Winnipeg, MB R3L 1L8
greatplainspress.ca

Great Plains Publications gratefully acknowledges the financial support provided for its publishing program by the Government of Canada through the Canada Book Fund; the Canada Council for the Arts; the Province of Manitoba through the Book Publishing Tax Credit and the Book Publisher Marketing Assistance Program; and the Manitoba Arts Council.

Design & Typography by Relish New Brand Experience
Printed in Canada by Friesens
Second printing, 2024

The Appendix contains information from the Manitoba government, licensed under the OpenMB Information and Data Use Licence (Manitoba.ca/OpenMB)

LIBRARY AND ARCHIVES CANADA CATALOGUING IN PUBLICATION

Title: Take your baby and run : how nurses blew the whistle on Canada's biggest cardiac
  disaster / Carol Youngson.
Names: Youngson, Carol, author.
Description: Includes index.
Identifiers: Canadiana (print) 20230466389 | Canadiana (ebook) 2023046646X | ISBN
  9781773371054 (softcover) | ISBN 9781773371061 (EPUB)
Subjects: LCSH: Youngson, Carol. | LCSH: Odim, Jonah. | LCSH: Health Sciences
  Centre (Winnipeg, Man.) | LCSH: Pediatric errors—Manitoba. | LCSH: Children—
  Manitoba—Death. | LCSH: Children—Hospital care—Manitoba. | LCSH: Pediatric
  cardiologists—Manitoba. | LCSH: Pediatric nursing—Manitoba. | LCSH: Whistle
  blowers—Manitoba.
Classification: LCC RJ47.2 .Y58 2023 | DDC 618.9200097127—dc23

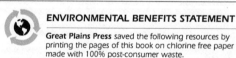

ENVIRONMENTAL BENEFITS STATEMENT

 Great Plains Press saved the following resources by printing the pages of this book on chlorine free paper made with 100% post-consumer waste.

TREES	WATER	ENERGY	SOLID WASTE	GREENHOUSE GASES
19	1,600	8	66	8,290
FULLY GROWN	GALLONS	MILLION BTUs	POUNDS	POUNDS

Environmental impact estimates were made using the Environmental Paper Network Paper Calculator 4.0. For more information visit www.papercalculator.org

Canadä

FSC
www.fsc.org
MIX
Paper | Supporting responsible forestry
FSC® C016245

Whenever a doctor cannot do good,
he must be kept from doing harm.

HIPPOCRATES

DEDICATED TO THE MEMORY OF:

Gary Caribou
Jessica Ulimaumi
Vinay Goyal
Daniel Terziski
Alyssa Still
Shalynn Piller
Aric Baumann
Marietess Capili
Erica Bichel
Ashton Feakes
Jesse Maguire
Erin Petkau

and their families

TABLE OF CONTENTS

FOREWORD

Author Carol Youngson and I have never met, yet our paths must have unknowingly crossed multiple times over the course of our careers.

Manitoba is a "big small town" and as graduates of the same school and one-time employees of the same hospital, Carol and I have no doubt shared many similar experiences throughout our careers. I was honoured to write this foreword to her book documenting a dark period in Manitoba's healthcare history.

Carol's book details her extraordinary experiences as lead operating room cardiac nurse during the catastrophic series of events that led to the untimely deaths of twelve young children. After three decades, Carol's account offers readers an insider's view of the tragic events and her own personal and professional struggles to support her patients and teammates amid the intense frustration she felt as her voice—and the voices of her colleagues—were muted. Although I do not know Carol personally, I feel a deep connection to her passion and her commitment.

Clinical providers are educated for careers dedicated to serving people during their most vulnerable moments. We train so we can manage high-risk, fast-paced, life-and-death situations. We develop skills in specialized areas and we learn to build bonds of trust with our patients and their loved ones. We do these things because they enable us to function proficiently as part of an integrated healthcare team. Most importantly, we commit ourselves to these efforts because we care and we want to make a difference in the lives of others.

In 1994, I was a third-year nursing student completing my clinical rotation on a pediatric medical unit at Health Sciences Centre Winnipeg's Children's Hospital. I was young, full of energy and optimism for the future. I was also blissfully unaware that just a few floors below me, in the operating room theatre within the same Manitoba hospital, a disaster was unfolding and a growing sense of dread was beginning to build amongst those closely involved with the pediatric cardiac surgery program.

Three years later, intense media coverage and the longest public inquiry in the history of our province had revealed the devastating details of how twelve children lost their lives undergoing cardiac surgery at HSC Children's. The inquiry's heart-wrenching account highlighted system failures and warning signs unheeded for too long.

By this time, I was a graduate, a registered nurse, and a mother of a newborn baby boy diagnosed with a cardiac condition. While I had previously followed media reports on the ongoing public inquiry with shock and disbelief, it had been from the distance of an outsider. Now, as I sat by my baby's bedside in the Pediatric Intensive Care Unit, I related on a personal level. After multiple invasive tests and interventions, we both had eyes swollen from crying and were exhausted. He was connected to so many monitors and machines that it was difficult for me to get close enough to comfort him. I was terrified to put my faith and trust in the experts who, although professional and kind, were strangers to me. I felt powerless to make him better and helpless as I watched my baby suffer.

I made choices for my child out of fear that there could be lingering dysfunctions within the now defunct pediatric cardiac surgery team. So many questions and scenarios went through my mind and I couldn't help but think of the parents of those twelve babies who came before mine— their fear, disappointment, pain, and fortitude to carry on.

Now, thirty years later, Carol Youngson's remarkable story reminds us of that dark time in our history. While Carol had graduated in 1969, at the height of the feminist movement, and was an expert nurse by 1994, she and her nursing colleagues functioned within a pervasive, patriarchal culture. Within this context existed a hierarchy of power and professional silos that proved to be key contributors to the crisis that was created.

The Operating Room environment is unlike any other, requiring at least three different healthcare professionals (anesthesiologist, nurse, and surgeon), dressed in matching attire, working in close proximity within a confined space for hours on end. With patients that are unconscious under anesthesia, the surgery team relies on protocols, technology, and skill to remove body parts, stop bleeding, repair damage, and save lives. There are multiple surgical specialties and every procedure, no matter how minor, carries some degree of risk.

Within the Operating Room theatres, every person has a defined role in order to fulfil a specific purpose. Concise communication is required, along with the ability to stay calm under pressure when things don't go as planned.

Looking back, it would be easy to point a finger and blame one villain. But in complex organisms like healthcare, the most wicked problems are multifactorial and thus, intricate and complex to solve. Judge Murray Sinclair, who presided over the Pediatric Cardiac Surgery Public Inquest, astutely acknowledged the many flaws that contributed to the deaths of the twelve children, including human error, unclear accountabilities, organizational structure, system processes, and overall culture. Like the Swiss Cheese Model of accident causation, multiple holes had to perfectly align in order to produce this magnitude of error.

The recommendations Sinclair delivered ensured safeguards were put into place to mitigate future risks of this nature, including revamping the Informed Consent process, passing whistleblower legislation and creating Nursing Practice Councils, where nurses can safely raise and formally escalate concerns without fear of retribution in the spirit of continuous improvement.

Clinicians who worked at the hospital during this time acknowledge how our health system changed after this event. Three decades later, the lessons that were learned will never be forgotten. For some, these lessons involved the need for critical evaluation, transparency of information, clear communication, mentorship, and careful selection of new medical recruits in order to ensure safety when establishing a high-risk, low-volume clinical service. For nurses in particular, it highlighted the worth of their role and the need to value and respect all individuals within a team. In healthcare, this also includes patients and their families. Strengthening collaboration and trusting partnerships within team-based models of care remains an ongoing priority of focus for healthcare organizations today.

As I embark upon my latest role as Chief Executive Officer within a complex provincial healthcare organization (that includes HSC Children's), I am humbled by the teams around me—their expertise, dedication and intentions to serve others well. Every day, they deliver excellent patient care that often goes unnoticed, and I trust them to guide my decisions and actions with their knowledge, evidence, and experiences. The magnitude of the challenges we face within healthcare can, at times, be daunting and overwhelming. And it can be tough to hear the issues raised by our teams; however, as leaders we owe it to our people and the populations we serve to listen, problem-solve together, and make the necessary decisions related to factors within our control.

Enabling high-functioning teams is the key to unlocking the magic of quality care. Carol's story offers a powerful reminder to all of us in healthcare to put our egos aside, be accountable for our individual actions, and base every decision on what is best for our patients and their families.

Today, my child and thousands of others have benefitted from the advocacy and learning of those who came before us. Manitoba children are now transferred out of province for pediatric cardiac surgical procedures, to centralized locations in neighbouring provinces. In locations where a higher volume of specialized procedures are performed, team expertise is enhanced, risks are lowered, and better health outcomes are realized. In my own family's care experience, our visit to Edmonton's Stollery Children's Hospital, 1,500 kilometres away, was completely coordinated through the Variety Children's Heart Centre. As a parent, I benefited from the trust and confidence I was able to have in the process and in the surgical team. Thanks to Justice Sinclair's recommendations, every detail was taken care of for us, dramatically reducing the stress we felt and allowing us to solely focus on our loved one.

Carol's book is a personal account of her own experience; however, it is worth reflecting on how everyone connected to this tragedy was required to carry their own burdens and find individual ways to cope and heal over time. For all those involved in the clinical care, the administration, and the public inquiry, this could not have been easy. But it was especially difficult for the parents and loved ones of the children involved and it is them we must keep top of mind well into the future as we pursue continuous improvement and give meaning to the lives lost and the grief endured.

For those who work in the broader healthcare sector, I encourage you to read this story of courage in the face of adversity thoughtfully. Let Carol's struggle be our inspiration well beyond the scope of pediatric cardiac surgery. Despite all we have learned in Manitoba, similar tragedies continue to occur in other jurisdictions where safeguards are lacking. This book serves as a reminder for all of us working within healthcare, everywhere, to stay grounded in our core principles, be brave enough to speak truth to power, value each member of our team, and always put patients first.

May we continue to forever honour the lessons that were learned, the burdens that were carried, and the hearts that were broken.

Lanette Siragusa, RN, MN
Winnipeg, July 2023

PREFACE

Erin Petkau was only three days old when she came into our operating room. She had been a full-term birth, but she was tiny, just 2.6 kg (about 5 lbs., 7 oz). We had warmed up the room and the bed for her. We tucked blankets around her, put a heating/cooling mattress under her and arranged a "Bair Hugger," a plastic blanket constantly filled with warm air from an attached blower, to keep her comfortable. But she was still just a little person on a huge operating table.

She was born on December 17, 1994, at the hospital in Morden, Manitoba. She was the only child of Walter and Barbara Petkau. On her second day of life, doctors identified a heart murmur and occasional blue spells, so she was transferred to our facility in Winnipeg, the Health Sciences Children's Centre. She was diagnosed with a complex congenital heart defect called Tetralogy of Fallot, as well as very small pulmonary arteries, severe pulmonary stenosis (blockage), and other anomalies. She would require major surgery when she was one or two years old.

A relatively simple palliative procedure called a Blalock Taussig Shunt (BT shunt) would redirect blood to her lungs right then, buying her some time to grow before the definitive repair could be done. Her pulmonary vessels, which take blood to the lungs, just weren't big enough to do the job.

The BT shunt procedure was usually considered an emergency and was often performed later in the day when the scheduled surgeries were finished. This was an operation we had done several times; another nurse, also named Carol (then McGilton, now Dupuis), had done many of them because she worked the 12:00 to 8:00 p.m. shift. We were both looking forward to Erin's case because it did not require putting the three-day-old infant on cardio-pulmonary bypass. In our experience with our previous cardiac surgeon, it usually took about three hours to do the BT shunt procedure with the patient leaving the OR in stable condition. We were hopeful.

That's not to say a BT shunt is not a serious operation. Any cardiac surgery is. But these patients usually did well. Erin came into the OR around 12:40 p.m. and the induction (the administration of the anesthetic and the insertion of lines) was begun. All cardiac patients need several monitoring lines inserted before surgery. Because Erin was so small, it was difficult to find an artery suitable for this. At some point, Dr. McNeill, the anesthetist, asked Dr. Jonah Odim, the surgeon, to perform a cutdown. A "cutdown" involves making a small skin incision at the location of an artery—in this case one in Erin's arm—and inserting the small line and suturing it in place. It is then connected to the cardiac monitor. It is secure throughout the procedure and the anesthetist can use it to read the blood pressure, heart rate measurements, blood gases and so on. As I stood beside Erin, watching Dr. Odim struggle to put in the line, I wondered why he was having so much trouble. Erin was a tiny baby, but he was a pediatric heart surgeon and should be skilled in this procedure. Sometimes this task is given to residents to perform. Finally, the line was in, sutured in place and a dressing placed on it.

From that point on, we positioned Erin, made sure she was properly covered, pressure points padded and all her lines in place. Monitoring equipment ran from her small body to machines at the head of the table where the anesthetist stood, a breathing tube down her throat was attached to a ventilator, and several IVs, medication pumps and other lines were running to and from her body, all for the one and only purpose of keeping her alive. Once we were satisfied that she was properly positioned and protected, she was covered with sterile drapes and the operation began.

Several people were present at that time. The anesthetist and her assistant at the child's head, Dr. Odim at Erin's side, his assistant, Dr. Betty Jean Hancock, across from him and the scrub nurse next to her. There were two circulating nurses (another RN and me) present as well. We moved around the OR keeping an eye on the surgeon and scrub nurse and providing them with any needed equipment. We also charted and documented all that occurred throughout the operation.

At 3:30 p.m., when my shift ended, despite all that had gone wrong in the previous eleven months, I felt comfortable enough to go home. We were not that far into it by then, but things seemed to be going smoothly and this was supposed to be a fairly simple procedure. This is normal during basic surgeries where another nurse comes on duty and relieves the one who is heading home. Had I been asked to, I would have stayed on, but Carol and the other nurses seemed to have everything under control. As well, I would have had to run it by my boss if I decided to stay overtime. That cost money!

However, after I left, things went wrong in a hurry (but not because I wasn't there). The BT shunt had not worked. It was too large, causing too much blood to flow into Erin's lungs, flooding them, with not enough blood going to her body. After a discussion with Dr. Niels Giddins, the cardiologist, Dr. Odim tied off the Patent Ductus Arteriosus, part of the fetal circulation which delivers oxygenated blood to the fetus before it is born and starts to breathe. This helped reduce the blood flow to the lungs. But every time Dr. Odim tried to close her chest, Erin's pressures and oxygen levels dropped. He re-examined the shunt. It was clotted. She would need another one.

This necessitated putting her on the bypass machine—a machine usually used during complex open-heart surgeries. It required inserting tubes called cannulas (venous and aortic) into the major vessels coming directly into the heart and taking the oxygen depleted blood from the patient via the venous cannula, running it through a membrane oxygenator and returning it with oxygen in it to the patient through the aortic cannula.

On an infant so small, it can be a very tricky and risky procedure and was highly unusual. In my experience, I knew it could happen, but I had never had a case where it did. This caused a significant delay while the room was set up. The perfusionists—the team of two technicians who ran the bypass machine—were paged, and equipment, instruments and sutures were added. Obviously, all this took time.

Erin finally went onto bypass at 7:30 p.m. but there were cannulation problems going on. The cannulas come in several different sizes and styles. It is up to the surgeon to determine which size and type of cannula to use. The perfusionists usually give him some assistance with that because they can calculate the patient's body surface area and advise him as to the blood flow requirements and size range from which to choose.

While placing Erin on bypass, it was determined that the venous cannula, which took blood from Erin to the bypass machine, was too small, so the flows were too low to sustain life. Most of the time a surgeon will use either two venous cannulas or what is known as a single "two-stage" cannula. The perfusionist thought Dr. Odim was going to use two venous cannulas and gave him the appropriately sized ones. However, the surgeon planned to use one and therefore should have asked for a two-stage cannula. Either method is acceptable, but it is important to know which one the surgeon wants to use. Dr. Odim failed to notice this and blamed the perfusionist for this error. The anesthetist said later that the surgeon should have known the cannula was too small. He was the one who had a good view of the heart and its vessels before inserting it. The cannula was changed, and the procedure went on. This was another example of the poor communication that was an ongoing problem throughout the year.

It was becoming difficult to keep Erin alive. The anesthetist was doing everything possible to keep her going. Her pressures and oxygen levels were dropping, and she was bleeding profusely. She was given meds, fluids and blood products; so much so that she received three times her total blood volume in the OR.

It took several attempts to wean Erin from the bypass machine and more than three hours to get her stable enough to close her chest. As they took off the sterile drapes, another problem presented itself. She had bled a huge amount from the cutdown that Dr. Odim had performed on her arm before surgery. The blood had soaked a large area of the sheet Erin lay on as well as the mattress beneath her. The cutdown had leaked. I had never seen or heard of this kind of blood loss from a cutdown.

Erin went to the Neonatal Intensive Care Unit (NICU) shortly after midnight. There followed many rounds of resuscitation in the NICU which included the surgeon reopening her tiny chest in the unit without the presence of the OR staff or an anesthetist. She was heavily sedated and would not feel any pain, but an anesthetist would be able to better monitor her throughout the procedure. Any member of the OR team, including me, would have come back to assist if called. Instead, it fell upon the NICU staff to assist in a difficult surgical procedure without the proper equipment or trained staff. This had been an ongoing problem throughout the year.

Despite heroic efforts, there was no way they could save her. Erin died in her mother's arms at 7:50 that morning, December 21, 1994.

As Erin's devastated parents stood at her bedside, Dr. Odim described in detail the nature of her problems and the issues that arose in the operating room. I doubt they absorbed much.

I learned all this when I came to work the next morning. I just stood there leaning against a wall in the hallway in silence, shocked and horrified by the news. When I left the OR the previous afternoon, I thought things were going well. *Should I have stayed?* Carol Dupuis was an experienced nurse. She and the others handled things well. I don't think my presence would have made any difference. But I wondered. *Could I have done anything? How could this have happened? What went wrong? Why couldn't the people in charge see what was going on?* The bigger question which came up later was *who was in charge?* It seemed so obvious to those of us who were witnessing it.

I was devastated. Then I cried.

ERIN PETKAU WAS THE LAST OF TWELVE CHILDREN TO DIE after having cardiac surgery in 1994 by our new pediatric cardiac surgeon, Dr. Jonah Odim, at the Children's Centre, part of Winnipeg's

Health Sciences Centre (HSC). This was once described to me as one of the greatest medical tragedies in Canadian history.

Erin's horrible death was ultimately ruled "possibly preventable" by Judge Murray Sinclair, who presided over the longest-running inquest in Canadian history. I would soon leave the nursing profession, haunted by five words I'd desperately wanted to say for most of that year as parents handed their tiny child to me: "*TAKE YOUR BABY AND RUN!*"

I have been told many times that I had a story to tell but life got in the way of doing so. I was working as an investigator for the Manitoba Department of Justice, in the Office of the Chief Medical Examiner after I left the OR in 1997. It was a demanding job with lots of overtime. And of course, I had family obligations. So I packed it all away, mentally, physically and emotionally. When I retired a few years ago, I finally had some time. My thoughts went back to the events of that year, and I wondered if controls were in place to ensure this would never happen again.

Then the COVID-19 pandemic arrived, and I saw our health care system, already in crisis, teetering on the edge of collapse. I finally felt ready to speak up.

This story will be told from my own recollections of the events of 1994 and the many repercussions and ramifications that followed over the subsequent years. I have used Judge Sinclair's report as a useful reference, and since it is online and in the public domain, it is a factual resource available for anyone to read. As well, I have reread many books, magazine and newspaper articles, TV interviews, court transcripts, and my own notes, all of which I saved in a box in my basement over the years. This book is told from my perspective as an experienced operating room nurse, what I saw, what I thought and how I felt during that terrible year. It's a story I feel needs to be told.

PART ONE
BEGINNINGS

CHAPTER 1

THE NURSE

I completed high school in Regina in June of 1966 and started a summer job babysitting two little boys. One day, my dad came over to the house where I was working, waving my Grade 12 final marks that had just arrived in the mail. "Four As, two Bs and a C," he said as he hurried up the walk.

Without looking at the report card, I knew the C was in Home Economics. Not my thing. I didn't mind the cooking part but sewing was a total disaster. I was more of a math and science person. I was good at figuring things out.

The grades were not a surprise to me, but I was still pleased for myself and happy for my dad. I knew it meant a lot to him because he was a school principal. Later that same summer, I left home to attend nursing school in Winnipeg. I was only eighteen years old, and I had lived my entire life with my parents in Saskatchewan. Now I was over five hundred kilometers away and incredibly homesick. Living in the nurses' residence with 150 classmates was in itself full of life lessons and taught me a lot about myself. I was able to overcome an almost pathological shyness and I made a lot of good friends. I am still close to many of my nursing school classmates.

When I was at home with my parents I had very little responsibility, but nursing is all about being responsible for others. I was learning the basics, including giving bed baths. This isn't as easy as it sounds. Bathing someone who is ill or in pain while they are still in their bed is tricky. The goal is a clean and dry patient as well as a clean and dry bed for them to lie in. Then there was learning how to make a bed, changing the sheets with the patient in it, preferably without dumping the patient on the floor in the process. I continue to make beds with "hospital corners" to this day.

During my nursing training, doctors were like gods. There was an unwritten rule that if a doctor entered the nursing station you were expected to stand and give him your chair. I was once reprimanded by a nursing instructor for failing to do just that. It was the late 1960s and the beginning of the women's movement. I knew doctors were much higher in the hospital hierarchy in those days, but even then, I felt that every member of the team had value and should be respectful of each other. If someone needed to sit for a reason such as fatigue, a disability or old age, I would happily give up my seat but just because this person had an MD behind his name didn't seem to be a good reason for me to jump out of my seat and stand when I might be in the middle of something important. I always tried to treat everyone with respect, but it wasn't always reciprocated.

When I finished the first of my three years of nurse training it was 1967, the "Summer of Love." Flower children were taking on the world. Women's rights were at the forefront. There were protest marches against the war in Viet Nam and against racism, and demands for equal rights. It was a time of tremendous change.

A wonderful photo entitled "Flower Power" was taken on October 21, 1967, of an eighteen-year-old man, believed to be George Harris, putting a flower into the end of a soldier's M14 rifle at a protest in Washington, DC. I have never forgotten that image. It was nominated for a Pulitzer. To me, that picture perfectly captured the zeitgeist of the late '60s— the struggle by the forces of change against the status quo. I admired the bravery of the young person who approached the soldier to do that, standing up to authority for something he really believed in. It would become personally relevant to me one day many years later.

I loved the '60s counterculture, the fashion, the long hair, and the music. I wore bell bottom pants and a fringed jacket, and my hair was almost waist long. More than anything, I wanted to be Janis Joplin; but sadly, I didn't have her voice. When I was deciding what to do with my life, the choices were limited. Young women where I came from had three primary options: nurse, teacher or secretary. My parents were both teachers, so I decided not to follow that path. Since I didn't want to work in an office, nursing was where I ended up.

To this day, I am not really sure why. Many of my nursing friends have said that they had always wanted to be a nurse. That wasn't me. But I had to do something, so because of my interest in science and math, I decided to give it a try. I was living the cultural revolution vicariously while I conformed to the ideals I had been raised to believe in: work hard, get an education, get married and have a family. I stayed the course and graduated from nursing school in 1969. Academically, it was easy. Clinically, not so much.

My first job was as a general duty nurse in a dialysis unit at the Winnipeg General Hospital (now known as the Health Sciences Centre). It was the early days of hemodialysis. I learned how to hook up patients and take them off of the dialysis machines, which were pretty basic back then. Later, I cared for the first kidney transplant patient in Manitoba. I had worked in the dialysis unit for a couple of years by then. I was still learning but could handle most of what was thrown at me. Then, I took a position in the Renal Outpatient Clinic at the same hospital, as an office nurse. I drew the patients' blood, checked their blood pressures, and after seeing the doctor, sent them on their way. The hours were great, but the pace was too slow. I was bored and I think it showed. I needed to be challenged. I wasn't keen on working a lot of shift work, so I took a job in the Children's operating room.

Initially, I wondered if it was the right decision. New situations scared and intimidated me, and there were lots of them coming at me in the operating room. The surgeons were especially scary. When a surgeon became angry, I found it very intimidating because back then they got away with a lot of bad behaviour. Yelling and abusive comments were common. Throwing instruments across the room happened from time to time. No one got hurt, at least not physically, but nurses had to suck it up and take it. I gained more confidence and developed a thicker skin. As time went by, bad behaviour became less acceptable and less frequent. One tactic that I heard of in later years was the "Code Pink." When a surgeon was becoming angry or abusive, a nurse in the OR theatre would call a Code Pink over the speaker system. Every available nurse would come to the theatre and stand there silently. No one said anything, but the tactic seemed to work.

The first cardiac surgeon I worked with was Dr. Colin Ferguson. We did simple cardiac cases, nothing too complex. It was still early days. He and the pediatric cardiologist Dr. Gordon Cumming had epic fights in the OR. The cardiologist would come into the OR to take cardiac pressures while the patient's chest was still open or at the end of the procedure. There often seemed to be some difficulty. Either the equipment wasn't functioning, or Dr. Ferguson didn't like the readings and would become impatient with Dr. Cumming and the row would begin. Somehow, they would figure it out, but not without some shouting and cursing. Both men were important for different reasons: Dr. Cumming would see and diagnose the patient, if they needed surgery, he would refer the patient to Dr. Ferguson. At that point in my career, I had no idea what the fights were about, but they were interesting to watch.

One of the most memorable people on that cardiac team was the perfusionist, Henry, who ran the cardio-pulmonary bypass machine. We had only one perfusionist those days. I am not sure what his background was. I think it had something to do with the animal research lab that was somewhere over in the Medical College. No one would talk about it. We just knew it existed.

Years later, it became mandatory to have two perfusionists present at every operation. Henry, whose last name I cannot remember, was very quiet and unassuming. He sat on a low stool behind his pump and rarely spoke to anyone but the surgeon. Henry was a Jehovah's Witness and often had to transfuse blood to our patients while they were on bypass. I guess his religious convictions didn't transfer to his professional duties. My most vivid memory of him was when I saw him crawling up the steps of the Children's Hospital on his hands and knees during an ice storm. We both made it in that day, although I think I managed to remain upright.

In the early '80s, my husband and I moved to Regina for three years. When we came back to Winnipeg, we had a toddler, so I took a part-time position back at Children's. Things had changed somewhat, but I slipped back into the routine fairly easily. There was some new equipment and procedures, and of course some of the staff had changed. But many of the same people were still there and it was an easy transition.

The OR offered many experiences—some were routine, others terrifying and some so tragic that words could never describe the intense feelings they generated. Our jobs were so important, so difficult, so heartbreaking, and yet so satisfying. Things went wrong for sure, tragedies happened, but miracles occurred too. Many of our patients weighed less than three pounds. Tiny little babies who were often so feisty, fighting for their lives. They were amazing little people.

Working in an OR was exhausting, physically and mentally, and by the end of the day I was tired and ready to go home. Sometimes I felt like a pawn on a chessboard, being moved around with little or no say as to which square I landed on. Surgery and anesthesia made all the decisions. As nurses we did as we were told, following the doctors' orders. But many children who might have died in previous eras were now living healthy lives thanks to medical intervention. I like to believe I played a part in that, and it kept me coming back to work every day. On occasion I would walk into the recovery room or into one of the ICUs to see what was going on. There would be children in their cribs, on stretchers or in isolettes (incubators), with the nurses watching over them as they recovered from surgery, their parents hovering nearby.

The most frightening thing for parents must have been handing their baby over to a complete stranger and trusting they would soon see that child in the recovery room. That is a giant leap of faith, one that I, as a parent, have had to do only once. I never took it for granted. Sometimes

I would glance back for a second as I carried a small child, often screaming in my arms, through the doors into the OR suite and see one or both
parents collapsing into tears. They had managed to put on a brave face
for their child, but the stress was too great to keep it together once their
child left with me.

We had a new cardiac surgeon by then, Dr. Kim Duncan. He had just
finished his training in England, and this was his first job. Since I had done
quite a bit of adult cardiac surgery in other hospitals by then, I expressed an
interest in doing pediatric cases and so within a few weeks, I was working
in Theatre 2, aka "The Heart Room." It was fun, exciting and rewarding
and I was happy to be back in that environment and doing that work again.
And so, when the nurse in charge left in 1991, I took her place and continued to do so until Dr. Duncan left for the United States in 1993. We
lost a few people around that time. They left for better opportunities in
larger centres in the United States or Canada. More money was a common
reason, although better working conditions, less call and better state of the
art equipment was also a draw. It was not just about a bigger paycheck.

For the most part, Dr. Duncan was fun to work with. He was originally from Edmonton, married with a family, and about the same age as
many of us on the cardiac team. He was a sports fan and he often talked
about the Winnipeg Jets or Blue Bombers, his kids' hockey games as well
as the latest *Seinfeld* episodes. We felt we had a lot in common with him.

When he first started in Winnipeg, he had his share of problems getting the cardiac program off the ground and building it to a level where
we as a team felt we were doing very good work. Fortunately, he had
a mentor, an older experienced cardiologist, Dr. George Collins, who
helped him decide which cases he should take on and which should be
sent out to larger centres, usually in Ontario. Dr. Collins kept his eye on
Dr. Duncan, even cancelling an operation occasionally when Dr. Duncan
had been up all night and was too tired to operate.

Like any cardiac OR, there was tension and stress, but we worked
well together. We were a team and several of us had been there for years.
We knew each other well and I think we all respected each other. I think
all of us felt a strong sense of belonging to a team.

Dr. Duncan could be difficult, but for the most part he was good to work with. From time to time, he would get angry and lash out. As the nurse in charge of that OR I usually heard about the issues that arose when I hadn't been in the room to witness them. I remember one nurse approaching me to tell me that he had been especially difficult one day. Later, I spoke to him about this and told him that the nurse involved was upset about his behaviour. He looked at me and said "Carol, what happens in the OR, ends there." To him, it was over and forgotten. Strong feelings were normal in this stressful environment. When it was over it was over. No hard feelings on his part. This wasn't always the way that the nurse on the receiving end of his comments felt. I don't think he ever apologized, but sometimes I would notice a softening of his behaviour the next time that person was there.

He stood up for members of his surgical team. We had several foreign residents who had come to Canada for training. Some of them would assist on one or two cardiac surgeries before moving on to another rotation. One day, I scrubbed in with Dr. Duncan. We had a Saudi resident assisting. As the operation progressed, I tried to hand the resident the necessary instruments. However, he ignored me and wouldn't always take them. Dr. Duncan noticed this out of the corner of his eye and eventually stopped what he was doing. He looked at the resident and said, "She has forgotten more about cardiac surgery than you will ever know. When she hands you something, fucking take it!" No trouble after that.

We often had music playing while we worked. Usually something light: pop, rock, or ballads. The music was on in the background and turned off whenever things got tense. Dr. Duncan's favourite was the "closing music" played at the end of the case as the chest was being sutured shut. The Traveling Wilburys' albums were often requested, and whenever I hear a tune from them, I think back fondly to those days.

Before Dr. Duncan left in 1993 for Omaha, a doctor from there came to observe him at work. He invited me to lunch that day so he could ask me about my experience working with Dr. Duncan. I think he wanted to know how Dr. Duncan got along with his team. As well, two nurses and a perfusionist came up to see how we did things, so they could better anticipate Dr. Duncan's needs and preferences. I thought this was very forward-thinking of his new hospital.

Admittedly, it saddened me to meet these people and know that they would be working with Dr. Duncan soon. I was trying to look forward to another surgeon taking his place, but we were used to working together as a team and now it was all going to change. I was sad to see him leave but I felt good assisting his transition to his new position. Before he left, he treated me and a couple of the other cardiac nurses to *The Phantom of the Opera,* which was touring and playing in Winnipeg at that time. Years later, on the hundredth anniversary of the establishment of the Children's Hospital in Winnipeg, he called me from Omaha and said he and his wife were coming for the celebration. He "bought" a table at the dinner and treated several of us again. He was a nice guy.

Soon after, Dr. Collins would depart for Ontario. He retired there and died a few years later. Change was coming and I was excited to be part of building on what we had accomplished so far. Little did I realize that our program would collapse under the weight of a tragedy that rocked us to our core, made national headlines, and resulted in the deaths of twelve children.

The following year would be the most difficult of my nursing career. I could never have imagined a situation where I would be treated like a hero one day and an idiot the next.

CHAPTER 2

THE SURGEON

When Dr. Duncan left Winnipeg, there were three cardiologists at the Variety Heart Centre. It was part of the Health Sciences Centre, located right across the street from the Children's Centre. Then Dr. Pelech left for the US and Dr. Collins for Ontario. So the department had just one very junior cardiologist, Dr. Niels Giddins.

Back in 1994, the Variety Children's Heart Centre was partially funded by the Variety Club, which made a commitment of $100,000 annually for several years, and with money from the public sector. The personnel, medical staff, and nurses were employees of the Health Sciences Centre.

The HSC began the search for another pediatric cardiac surgeon. I had no part in the selection process. First up, a female cardiac surgeon came from the States for a visit. She was arrogant, full of herself, and made it clear to me that she planned to bring her own assistant (nurse) with her. I could see problems ahead. Thankfully, she didn't make the cut.

The next candidate I met was Dr. Jonah Odim. He was originally from Nigeria but had lived and been educated in the United States and Canada for years. His father was a famous doctor who had saved many

lives during the wars that occurred in Africa at the time. He came with
stellar Ivy League credentials, including a fancy prep school, a medical
degree from Yale, general surgical training in Chicago, cardiovascular-
thoracic surgical training at Montreal's McGill University, one year of
pediatric cardiac surgery at Montreal General Hospital followed by three
years of research, and finally, further training in pediatric cardiac surgery
at the world-renowned Boston Children's Hospital affiliated with Harvard
University. All this and a twenty-five-page CV! Everyone, including me,
was very impressed.

He had been recruited by Dr. Robert Blanchard, HSC's chief of surgery and Dr. Helmut Unruh, a thoracic surgeon. He had three reference
letters. One was from a Dr. Chiu, who had initially recommended him
to Dr. Unruh at a conference they both attended. The second letter was
from Dr. Mulder, who worked with Dr. Odim at McGill. He described
good leadership and surgical skills. He went on to say in a second letter
that technically he was not as mature as some of the other residents but
at the completion of his training he was a competent cardiothoracic surgeon. He suggested that Dr. Blanchard contact Dr. Aldo Casteneda, who
had been Dr. Odim's supervisor, in Boston. Dr. Blanchard attempted to
do that but was never able to reach Dr. Casteneda, who was out of the
country at the time.

Another letter written by Dr. Tchervenkov, a pediatric cardiac surgeon from Montreal who trained Dr. Odim, wrote what would later
seem prophetic: "As far as training goes, he has certainly had more than
enough. As far as whether he can really be successful at today's pediatric
cardiac surgery approach, that is always the question for anyone until
they actually prove themselves. I have seen what were considered excellent surgeons with excellent training in pediatric cardiac surgery bomb
out." I often wonder why no one paid attention to it at the time. Were
they all star-struck by Dr. Odim's credentials? I was told over and over
again that this candidate was highly qualified and that we were lucky
to get him. We all thought that he was going to take us to another level.

So I was told the general consensus within the search committee
was that we had a brilliant candidate. This was Winnipeg. Our medical

system was well-known and well-regarded in Canada, but this guy was from Boston. We figured he knew it all. We had very high expectations. He was from a place we assumed was the pinnacle of medical research and patient care. He had attended Yale and other Ivy League schools and yet no one wondered why someone with this background would want to come to Winnipeg. I know I never gave it a thought at the time, although much later I questioned it and was told that Dr. Odim had stated he wanted to make his mark and be a big fish in a small pond. This was his first job.

I often wonder if hiring Dr. Odim was an attempt to put the Health Sciences Centre on the map as far as pediatric cardiac surgery was concerned. I guess if Dr. Odim had lived up to those expectations, I wouldn't be writing this now. Sadly, he put us on the map for an entirely different reason.

Dr. Odim was a dapper guy in his late thirties or early forties. He was extremely fit, muscular and wore fancy suits, pocket hankies, crisp shirts and bowties. Although doctors often wore suits, this was on another level. Personally, I thought the bowties were a bit much for a young man… more of an old guy thing, I thought, and maybe that was my first clue there might be trouble. It seemed somewhat pretentious in his first big job, at least for a doctor on the Canadian prairies, but I'm sure he wanted to make a good impression.

He seemed pleasant enough. I was asked to meet him since he was the potential successful candidate and I was the nurse in charge of the cardiac operating room at Children's. The negotiations were still going on when we met, but I was told that he was likely going to take the job. We met for lunch at a restaurant near the hospital. I asked and answered many questions.

I mentioned that I needed some input about his surgical preferences— there was money allotted to buy some new instruments and equipment and would he sit down with me and go through some medical catalogues and pick out whatever he needed? I said I was available almost anytime.

He chuckled and said that whatever we had used before with Dr. Duncan would be fine. He would adapt as he went along, and I was not to worry. I remember thinking, *Well this is different, a surgeon who doesn't have his own special preferences for instruments, sutures etcetera!* Surgeons are usually very particular and have definite likes and dislikes. I chalked it up to him trying to be agreeable and fit in, but I still felt uneasy about this. I really wanted to get a handle on what he used. I wanted specifics. Which instruments, sutures, cannulas did he want? I asked him if he wanted to have a look at our instrument sets to see the cardiac instruments in particular. For example, there are several clamps that have specific uses during these surgeries. Different sizes, depending on the size of the child. Would he like to check them, make sure he was familiar with their names and uses? Nope. Not interested. I had never met a surgeon who didn't have strong opinions about what he liked to use when operating and it certainly wasn't up to me to decide this. In fact, it was unheard of for a nurse to make these types of decisions. It made me nervous. Once in a while, we made suggestions but usually it was some small change based on what we were already working with. I often met with sales reps who would sometimes give me samples of sutures to try. Occasionally, I would show them to a surgeon and often they would refuse to try them. They didn't like to change things. If it isn't broken, don't fix it. But these were things that were tried and true. Because our team had worked so well together for the past few years, I felt confident that with the help of anesthesia and perfusion, our first few cases could go smoothly, and we would learn as we went along. I trusted him. He was a doctor. He was smart. He had these great credentials after all.

I did have a plan. I had saved Dr. Duncan's preference cards. These were like little "recipe cards," one for each surgery a surgeon would perform. When preparing for an upcoming operation, a nurse or technician goes to the instrument room and picks out the applicable card. There was a standard set of instruments, but each doctor had a few extra instruments that they liked, and these were added to the set. Also, the sutures were picked and set aside along with any other equipment required. Some surgeons had long lists of special requests, others had very few. So, armed with these preference cards and my plan to create new ones for Dr. Odim as we went along, I felt I was ready to begin working with him.

At first, Dr. Odim seemed grateful and impressed with my knowledge and skill. In fact, at one point early on, he mentioned that he thought I should scrub for all his cases for the first six months or so. I was flattered and thanked him and told him that while I enjoyed scrubbing for these big cases, other nurses needed to get experience too. I might be on vacation or sick, or my child might be sick. There could be any number of reasons why I might not be there, and it wouldn't be fair to the other nurses or to him not to let them gain some experience. This practical response seemed to make no sense to him. Although he never asked why I would stay home if my child was sick or why I would take vacations, I got the impression that he questioned my dedication to my job. My reasons for not agreeing would come back to bite me.

"Scrubbing" for surgery involves a lot of things. The scrub nurse sets up the operating room for the patient, getting the instruments and tools necessary and making sure that sterile technique is maintained throughout the operation. We "scrub"—wash our hands and arms up our elbows with special antibacterial soap for a specified amount of time—don sterile gowns and gloves, set up the tables that hold all the sterile instruments and equipment, drape the patient, gown and glove the surgeon and assistant(s), hand the necessary instruments to the surgeon and assistant and try to anticipate their needs. On the back table I used to set up for open-heart surgeries, there were between one to two hundred instruments. They all had a name. When the surgery was completed, the circulating nurse and I would make sure everything was accounted for. All sutures, sponges, and instruments were counted prior to the first incision and again before the last stitch went in. Legally, it had to be correct. I usually applied the dressing. I signed off the count sheet and any other documents and assisted in transferring the patient to the stretcher or bed. Lastly, I rolled a cart with all the used and dirty equipment to the "clean up room" where a health care aide washed and sterilized them.

One of the things that we, as a team, did prior to an elective cardiac operation was to have a meeting, called cardiac rounds, with all concerned. They were attended by anyone who was involved in the care of the patient or interested in learning. HSC is a teaching hospital affiliated with the

University of Manitoba. I was expected to attend these meetings. Also in attendance was the surgeon, anesthetists, residents, pediatric cardiologists, referring pediatricians, intensivists, nurses from other disciplines (Pediatric Intensive Care Unit, Neonatal Intensive Care Unit, Variety Heart Centre, surgical wards), social workers, perfusionists, medical students and others. The patients who were slated for surgery in the next few days were discussed. X-rays, ultrasounds, cardiac catheterization results, and other information were shown. Everyone knew what they were dealing with and hopefully there would be no surprises. Usually, the patient had been seen several times by the nurses and doctors in the Variety Heart Centre and a care plan was in place. Plans could change of course. Emergencies arrived at the hospital from time to time. Nothing was written in stone, but we all had a basic idea of who was coming and what was going to happen in the OR. This was what had taken place routinely for several years and certainly helped me plan my part in the surgery. Questions were asked and answered, and the care of the patient was discussed.

My duties as a cardiac OR nurse were mainly to help the surgeon in the planning of operations and assisting with the surgical procedures. I would order supplies and make sure that the necessary instruments were available in the OR. The sutures needed for the operation were picked and in the room. Any other items, such as specialized equipment needed for a particular operation, were included. This is where the surgeon's preference cards were so valuable. The patient's X-rays were in the OR and up on the viewer. Everything that was needed for a successful surgical outcome was there at the ready, even items that *might* be needed were nearby, ready to be opened and used.

Lastly, I was tasked with teaching other nurses how to scrub and circulate for these cases. A lot of nurses were intimidated by the thought of assisting with cardiac surgical cases. There was a lot to remember, and things could go wrong in an instant.

Anesthesia needed an assistant too, although there was almost always an anesthesia resident in the OR. Irene Hinam was the nurse assigned to help them. She was a PICU nurse with years of experience, and she worked with anesthesia on all difficult and complex cases: setting up IVs, getting equipment, monitors, and ventilators ready and assisting in putting in several monitoring "lines" and IVs. They are all necessary for the precise monitoring of the patient's vital signs during and after surgery. Irene stayed around throughout the operations, coming in and out of the theatre to see if the anesthetist needed anything. If things weren't going well, she stayed in the OR and helped with blood transfusions, meds, and anything else that was required. She was also the liaison with the intensive care units. She would update them throughout the day and as an operation was winding down, would alert the ICU that the patient was coming to their unit and tell them what monitoring lines and devices were in place. That way they were ready. Irene knew her job and was very good at it.

Then there were "The Boys"—Mike Maas, Todd Koga, Dave Smith, and Chris McCudden. They were the perfusionists who ran the heart-lung machine that performed the life-sustaining cardio-pulmonary bypass. They came in pairs; they were usually the first to arrive in the OR early in the morning and were busy setting up their machines when the nurses showed up. Most had been respiratory therapists or nurses in their previous careers and had received extensive training to run and monitor the bypass machine. Essentially, their machine took over the work of the heart and lungs to keep the patient oxygenated and alive while the repair was being performed. The surgeon counted on them to make sure the patient was receiving oxygenated blood throughout the repair phase of the surgery. They had a lot of responsibility, and they knew their stuff.

During the surgery, everyone had their position and it rarely varied. The anesthetist was at the head of the bed where all the monitors were and where he or she could monitor the patient's vital signs and access the airway. On the patient's right stood the surgeon, with me, the first scrub nurse, next to him on his right. On the other side of the patient, opposite the surgeon, was the first assistant, usually Dr. Hancock. Next to her, on her left was either another assistant, perhaps a surgical resident, or a med student there to observe. Finally, the second scrub nurse stood directly across from me. A large high table was pushed in over the patient's legs and it contained all the instruments and sutures that we would need. Both scrub nurses stood on high platforms so they could see over the shoulders of the surgeon and the assistant. The two perfusionists sat on low stools behind their pump, which was situated behind the surgeon.

This was a well-oiled machine. We were a team, and after years of working together, we all knew our roles. Most of the time we actually had fun. We were all anticipating working with this new surgeon with the stellar credentials. We spoke about it often, and at some point someone suggested we have a "dry run," where everyone would participate and Dr. Odim, who was essentially the captain of the ship, would see how things were done. We wanted to make sure the first case went smoothly, for the sake of the patient, and of course, we wanted to impress our new surgeon.

The next time I saw him, I suggested the dry run to him. Again, I was met with resistance "We can just do what you always did with Dr. Duncan," he said. He was not interested in a dry run, it seemed. Again, this was new and not typical for a cardiac surgeon. It was puzzling. They are dealing with life and death situations and want to make sure things are done their way. They like to get to know the environment and their staff. All that happened was a brief tour of the cardiac theatre with Dr. Odim; one of the perfusionists, Chris McCudden; and me. We showed him some cannulas, sutures and other supplies and he seemed satisfied.

So no dry run.

I cannot say I felt completely ready. All I knew was what we had experienced before with Dr. Duncan and some of my previous experiences with adult cardiac cases. I knew every surgeon was different, but the sequence of events during cardiac surgery was pretty much the same for everyone. That much I was comfortable with. Open the chest, go on bypass, do the repair, come off bypass and close. Go home. I'd seen it done literally hundreds of times on adults and children. What I wasn't prepared for mentally was the stress of dealing with someone who seemed, in my opinion, unable to perform the basics of cardiac surgery, such as cannulation, let alone the complex repairs he attempted. You cannot fake surgical skill. You cannot fake "good hands." You might have a head-full of medical knowledge and be able to talk the talk, but a surgeon has to also be able to walk the walk.

In the year that followed Dr. Odim's arrival, I was to find out that no matter how hard I tried to make things run smoothly, things went wrong. Tragedy after tragedy occurred. I went from being impressed with Dr. Odim's credentials to wondering if he actually had a medical degree. *Was he an imposter? Had he stolen someone's credentials?* It gnawed away at me. Maybe he never even went to medical school. Or perhaps he had not completed his training. I had no one to ask and it would have sounded crazy anyway. I had to accept the fact that he was qualified. The hospital had hired him, they must have checked his references. For such an important position, he must have been thoroughly vetted. I had to believe in the system.

ON MARCH 7, 1994, the team did Dr. Odim's first open-heart case, where the child would be placed on cardio-pulmonary bypass. She was a little Indigenous girl, about seven years old. Her diagnosis was atrial septal defect (ASD), which is a hole between the right and left atria, the upper two chambers of the heart. This is one of the more common congenital defects and sometimes it closes on its own with no surgical intervention. Those that don't close require an operation that involves opening the chest through the sternum, inserting the bypass cannulas and going on bypass briefly. By the late 1990s, most ASDs were closed by a transcatheter technique.

This is a fairly simple operation as pediatric cardiac surgeries go. It usually takes two or three hours, start to finish, if all goes well. Since it was our first case it took somewhat longer, which was what I would have expected. The child entered the OR at 12:28 p.m. and left for PICU at 5:17 p.m. After a few tense moments draping and setting up the equipment in the sterile field, we got things underway.

Right away, Dr. Odim, who had previously stated he would "go with the flow," started changing things. He criticized the draping procedure, wanting small changes made. I didn't like the new system much as our old procedure had worked well, but I let it go. There was a pack of sterile tubings (lines) that rested on the patient's legs which were, by now, covered with sterile drapes. One end would be handed off to the perfusionist to attach to the bypass machine behind the surgeon. Dr. Odim didn't like the location of the tubing and wanted it changed, but the perfusionists stepped in and advised him that the lines had to go off the sterile field in a certain location to connect to the pump, so he backed down on that. At the time these seemed to be minor things, but they proved to be signs of problems to come. I felt that he was asserting himself, being the "captain of the ship," and at this point I was okay with that. However, more serious surprises were on the way.

One of the things I remember during this first case was that Dr. Odim did not seem to be comfortable with the cannulation procedure and had some difficulty with both the venous and arterial cannulations. His technique seemed rough to me, and he made a couple of attempts at each cannulation, at one point cutting through a "purse string" suture with the scalpel. The purse string is a little circular series of stitches the surgeon puts in the top surface of the blood vessel that will be cannulated. The suture ends are left long, and when it's time to insert the cannula, a tiny hole is made in the middle of the circle of stitches through which the cannula is quickly inserted. The sutures are then tightened around the tip of the cannula like a purse string. The purse string ends are then secured with a clamp and loosened when it's time to remove the cannula, then tightened to close the hole in the vessel and tied off. Dr. Odim seemed not to have mastered this skill, a basic one for a cardiac surgeon, it seemed to me, one he should have done over and over. He inadvertently cut through the purse strings on many occasions during several subsequent operations. These are major vessels coming directly out of the heart, which means that as he attempted to cut into the vessel prior to inserting the cannula and cut through the purse string, there was an immediate and significant blood loss that could be difficult to control. This was very surprising and disconcerting to all of us. There was a scramble to transfuse the patient, make sure another suture was placed and that the cannula secured.

Initially, I thought this was a problem that happened because it was our first case. I gave him the benefit of the doubt. Maybe he was unfamiliar with our ways, or nervous…whatever, but it would happen over and over again throughout the year. After seeing this occur during the first couple of cases, I made sure I always had three or four extra sutures on my table at all times in case I would need them quickly. Later, I wondered if he had a problem seeing. Maybe his headlight wasn't positioned correctly or his loupes weren't focused. *How could he keep cutting through the purse strings and damaging the vessels?* I had never seen that before in the many cases I had been involved with.

There weren't too many other mishaps or bumps in the road in this case and the child went to the PICU overnight in stable condition. She went home a few days later.

There was one other incident that foretold another kind of problem that we would be facing that year. At the beginning of the case, a nasty shock was in store for the other scrub nurse and me. I cannot reveal what Dr. Odim said, but it was extremely unprofessional and disrespectful to the two of us as women. I was shocked and surprised at what he said, and wondered if I'd heard it correctly. The other nurse, Carol Dupuis, and I spoke of it later. We both heard it, as did several other people present at the time. We let it go at that point, chalking it up to someone who was nervous and trying to make a joke. There was before the #MeToo and Time's Up movements. We never forgot it though. At the end of the day, we all breathed a sigh of relief. The first case was done and the child was okay. That was what mattered most.

Over the course of the next eleven months, according to a letter he later wrote to his medical colleagues, Dr. Odim operated on seventy-eight children, including forty-four pump (open) cases and thirty-four non-pump cases. Some were relatively minor cases, some complex and high-risk. Several who survived suffered severe complications, during and after surgery, including one child who now has permanent paralysis from the waist down.

Twelve died.

Most of the large surgical centres have mortality rates of between two to four percent. Of course, there are several things factored in these findings, including the number of children who are operated on, the ages and sizes of the kids, low- verses high-risk. Larger centres did more cases, and many studies conclude that the higher the volume of cases the centre and the surgeon perform, the lower the mortality rates. Lower centre and surgeon volume rates are associated with higher in-hospital mortality. It made sense.

Winnipeg was not a high-volume centre. Manitoba's population was not high enough for the HSC to have a large number of surgical patients, even with referrals from northwestern Ontario and Saskatchewan from time to time.

Many centres use the STAT category method, developed by the Society of Thoracic Surgeons in the late 1990s, to evaluate their survival rates. The STAT categories classify heart surgeries into groups based on complexity and operative risk, STAT 1 category being surgeries with the lowest risk of death, and the STAT 5 category indicating the surgeries with the highest risk of death.

As an experienced OR nurse doing cardiac and other high-risk procedures, I saw children die from time to time. No one ever gets used to it, but as professionals we learn to cope. It was *how* these twelve children died that was so unsettling: long bypass times resulting in issues with bleeding, cardiac failure, repairs failing and having to be redone, pacing problems. All were complications we saw on a regular basis in 1994.

CHAPTER 3

GARY CARIBOU

Gary was a tiny Indigenous baby. He was born on August 22, 1993, and lived on the Mathias Columb Cree Nation (aka Pukatawagan), about 1,000 km north of Winnipeg. His parents had lived there for their entire lives.

Manitoba is a large province in the middle of Canada. Most of its 1.3 million people live in the south, within two to three hundred kilometers of the US border. The northern part is sparsely populated with small towns and Indigenous communities. Many of these reserves are accessible only by air and by ice roads in the winter. On-reserve medical care is funded by the federal government for the most part, and the clinics are usually nursing stations staffed by nurses with extensive training in urgent care or nurse practitioners and a doctor who flies in on a regular basis. Emergencies are dealt with by them and if further care is required, the patient is flown to a larger urban centre.

Gary's mother took him to their nursing station a few weeks after his birth, when he started having breathing problems. He was diagnosed with pneumonia and started on antibiotics. Over the next few weeks, he continued to have difficulties and he spent a month or so in the hospital in the town of Lynn Lake before being flown to Winnipeg with a suspected heart problem. There he was seen by Dr. Niels Giddins, who diagnosed a VSD.

A VSD, or ventricular septal defect, is a hole between the right and left ventricles, the main pumping chambers of the heart. It often leads to other problems with the pressures within the heart and lungs, to breathing problems, and sometimes to death. It is a serious condition. Sometimes the hole, if it is small, will close on its own over time. In Gary's case it was large and allowed excessive blood to the lungs through the VSD. It impeded his ability to feed and grow. He just wasn't strong enough to suck enough milk to gain weight. Tube feedings were tried, and he seemed to do a bit better until they tried to increase the volume of the feeds. He vomited. So it was a bit of a catch-22. For him to be in optimal condition for surgery, he needed to grow. However, he couldn't grow if he didn't eat, and that was a problem because of his heart condition. He just didn't have the strength. This was discussed with his mother, Charlotte, and on December 27, 1993 he was returned to the Lynn Lake Hospital for further care. He did not do very well though and wasn't able to feed and gain weight, so in February 1994, he returned to Winnipeg.

He was admitted to the Children's Centre and seen by Dr. Giddins and Dr. Odim at the Variety Heart Centre. Gary's situation was discussed with the team. The concern was whether he was strong and healthy enough to withstand the surgical procedure. He suffered from "failure to thrive," a condition in children where they don't grow and develop normally because of some factor, including heart problems, as in Gary's case. He was small, underweight, and very frail. Dr. Odim stated that Gary would most likely have a very rocky post-operative course. However, after weighing all the pros and cons, the decision was made to operate, and Gary was taken to the OR on March 14, 1994.

It is not clear if Gary's mother was fully aware of the situation. It was explained to her that Gary had a hole in his heart and that he needed an operation to fix it. Although English was not her first language, the doctors felt that they had adequately explained everything in terms that she could understand. And so she signed the consent to operate. Later, she said that she deferred all the decisions for her son's care to the doctors. They knew best, in her opinion, and she trusted them.

In the days immediately before the surgery, Gary developed increased wheezing, a runny nose, and other respiratory issues. However, without the surgery, his future was at risk. There were many discussions as to the cause of Gary's respiratory problems. Some doctors thought it was due to his heart condition and therefore surgery was the answer, while others believed it was due to reactive airway disease or an infection. There were differences in opinion between the physicians who cared for Gary as to whether his surgery should be delayed due to his lung condition. Dr. Giddins and Dr. Odim discounted the possibility of Gary having a respiratory infection, although there were no tests recorded to support this. However, their belief that Gary's respiratory problems and failure to thrive would not improve until he had surgery was reasonable. Whatever the reason, he was not in top shape for surgery. As far as I know, none of this was discussed with his parents.

Gary's operation was difficult and long. He entered the OR at 12:15 p.m. Total surgical time was seven hours and forty-one minutes. At the beginning, when Dr. Odim was about to open Gary's sternum (or breastbone), he asked me for the pneumatic power saw. Gary was so tiny, his sternum was still thin and soft, and other surgeons I had worked with used scissors to cut through it. A safer option, I believed. I didn't even have the requested tool on my table. Stunned, I asked Dr. Odim why he needed the saw and his reply to me was "Because it makes me feel like a man." This was not the answer I was expecting. It seemed sarcastic and inappropriate. I gave him the saw.

The repair took longer than normal, I thought, because Dr. Odim used an interrupted suturing method of sewing in the patch, rather than a running, continuous stitch. This was a problem as the sutures repeatedly became tangled. Gary came off bypass with decent hemodynamics (heart rate and blood pressure). His chest was closed but shortly before he left the OR, his blood pressure fell. Dr. Odim reopened his chest, which immediately improved things. It was noted that there was a lot of tissue swelling within his tiny chest cavity. This would usually resolve in a few days, at which time he would go back to the OR briefly to have his chest closed. A piece of silastic (medical grade elastic sheeting) was placed over the incision and a dressing applied and Gary went to the

PICU at 9:55 p.m. When there is a problem with hemodynamics after cardiac surgery whereby the sternum cannot be closed, it can often be due to long bypass times. Gary's was three hours and forty-six minutes, which is considered long, especially for a small child. This can cause myocardial (heart muscle) damage and swelling.

Gary had a rocky post-operative course in the intensive care unit. During his first post-operative night, he had several cardiac arrests. He was bleeding and multiple boluses (small transfusions) of blood products were given.

Early the following morning, Dr. Odim decided to close Gary's chest. In the past, this procedure had been done in the OR, where there was properly trained staff and dedicated equipment. But Dr. Odim insisted on doing it in the PICU, much to the consternation and strong objections of the PICU nursing staff. These nurses felt they did not have adequate warning and supplies. In the past, Dr. Duncan had always given the staff plenty of warning if he planned to do any kind of procedure in the unit. Most of the time he preferred to take patients to the OR, which was the safer option. It is difficult for the staff, moving a critically ill child, but we all helped out and made it happen. In the worst-case scenario, if there was no way to transfer a critically ill child safely, the OR staff would come to the ICU to assist. We brought our supplies, instruments, sutures and a cart full of equipment, trying to foresee any complication that might arise.

However, Dr. Odim insisted and went ahead, despite the objections of Donna Feser, the nurse in charge, who was "flabbergasted" by this decision. He closed Gary's chest without any OR staff present. Also, no anesthetist was present, which is a potentially dangerous situation. The doctor in the PICU now had to stay with Gary, thereby making himself unavailable to the other patients in the unit. To this day, I still can't understand how Dr. Odim didn't get that.

A few days after that incident, I spoke to Dr. Odim about doing these procedures in the ICUs. I explained that the nurses there were not comfortable doing this. They didn't have the training to provide surgical assistance, just as I didn't have the training to look after a child in the

PICU. He told me in no uncertain terms not to insult the intelligence of the PICU nurses. Somehow, he seemed to think that I was criticizing or demeaning them. I was confused because I was actually sticking up for them. They had come to me asking for help and information about what supplies they should have in their unit in case this happened again. They were scared and now Dr. Odim was telling me not to underestimate or insult them.

I concluded, based on this and other incidents throughout that year and the fact that Dr. Odim could never seem to find the time to meet with me or the other nurses, that he really had no respect for us as a professional body. I don't think he knew or cared that nurses are specialists in their respective fields. I would never dare look after a child in the PICU. I don't have the knowledge or training to do it safely. Similarly, an ICU nurse could never do my job without some extra training. However, it seemed to me that Dr. Odim thought we were all interchangeable. A nurse is a nurse is a nurse. At some point later on, I put together a list of supplies and the PICU nurses and I made up a "cardiac bin" to keep in the PICU in case this happened again. It contained sutures, pacing wires, dressings, and other items that might be needed. My recollection is that Dr. Odim played no part in this. If he did, I was not aware.

GARY DEVELOPED RENAL FAILURE and peritoneal dialysis was attempted. This was a procedure where a small catheter is inserted into the abdomen and a special solution is run in. By osmosis, it absorbs the waste products in the blood that the kidneys usually take away, and then it is drained away out of the abdomen. During this procedure Gary's blood pressure dropped, and after an unsuccessful resuscitation, he died at 10:09 p.m. on March 15, 1994.

I don't remember how I felt about Gary's death. In my experience back then, we hadn't lost a patient with a VSD in recent memory. He died in the PICU, and I heard about it later. He was the first of the twelve children to die, and because he was so frail, I think I accepted it as one of the small number of children who don't make it after this type of surgery. I was sad though. He was such a tiny, frail little guy.

CHAPTER 4

JESSICA ULIMAUMI

Jessica was born August 18, 1993 in the Arviat Health Centre in the Northern territory of Nunavut. Not long after her birth, a nurse noted a loud heart murmur, which was confirmed by a visiting physician who referred her to a pediatrician in Winnipeg. She was seen at The Variety Heart Centre at about six weeks of age and was diagnosed with an ASD, VSD, and mild tricuspid valve regurgitation. All these defects were serious and alarming, and Jessica could not survive long without surgical intervention.

Over the next few months, Jessica was seen several times by medical personnel, including HSC cardiologist Dr. Giddins. In March 1994, a decision was made to operate on Jessica. She was still not in optimal condition. She had respiratory distress and was not really gaining weight, leading to a diagnosis of "failure to thrive." She was admitted to the hospital in Churchill on March 18 with nausea, vomiting, diarrhea, and fever, and diagnosed with gastroenteritis. She was transferred to Winnipeg, and on March 24, despite having a chest X-ray which showed signs of congestion which could mean she had a chest infection, she went to the OR for her repair. Again, we were dealing with a tiny, pale, underweight infant who was not in optimal shape for surgery.

The operation was long and difficult. Her bypass time was eight hours and forty-three minutes. This was very, very long. The surgery lasted thirteen hours and thirty-three minutes. A patch was sutured over the VSD, and it was noted as attempts were made to wean Jessica off the bypass machine that it was leaking. Dr. Odim commented to me that if he had had the right kind of suture, this wouldn't have happened. This was upsetting to me as I felt he was blaming me for the failure of the repair. His complaint was just what I had tried to avoid by repeatedly asking him for input regarding equipment, including sutures, back in February. He was using what we had always used, which was what he had previously told me would be fine. I was certainly willing to order other types of sutures for him. He never asked. In my opinion, the problem wasn't the suture, it was the suturing. It was also the beginning of a pattern of blaming others when things went wrong.

The repair had to be redone, which meant going back on bypass. This was very hard on such a tiny child, but we had no choice. Later, her heart displayed signs of being "stunned" by the lengthy bypass and cross-clamp times (8 hours and 43 minutes and 2 hours and 7 minutes respectively) during which the heart was arrested and not beating. It could not sustain life and so the decision was made to put Jessica on Extra Corporeal Membrane Oxygenation (ECMO), a form of bypass that would allow her to go to the PICU and rest her heart for a day or two. This was a complex and dicey situation, and it meant that one of the perfusionists had to be present at all times in the PICU to run the machine and watch for problems.

Whenever we do surgical procedures, it is the responsibility of two nurses, the scrub and the circulator, to make sure that all needles, sponges, and instruments are counted. These items are counted before we begin, documented on a count sheet and anything added or subtracted throughout the procedure is also counted in or out. Once the surgeon announces that the chest can be closed, a count of every item is begun and must be completed. A nurse will announce that the count is correct. In big complex cases, the surgeon will often ask how the count is coming along and will not proceed with closing if something is missing. Many of the needles are tiny, only millimeters long, and can be easily lost. We had magnetic boards to place used needles on which made it easier to keep track of them. If something was missing at the end and, after a thorough search was done, it could not be located, the surgeon would, according to hospital policy, order an X-ray to see if the item showed up on it. An incident report would be filled out and signed by the nurses involved and by the surgeon. Over the years, I have spent many minutes crawling around on the floor with a magnet, asking the surgeon and the assistants to lift their feet so I could see the soles of their shoes while I looked for a lost needle.

At the end of Jessica's surgery, a needle was missing. We did a thorough search and could not find it. Dr. Odim was notified but he declined to have an X-ray taken in the OR, stating that Jessica was too unstable at the time. So Jessica went off to the PICU. It was Thursday night. I finally got to go home.

Jessica's post-operative course in PICU was very difficult. She arrived in the intensive care unit accompanied by several doctors and nurses. Because of her many transfusions and long pump run, she had what is known as a positive fluid balance. She had too much fluid in the tissues of her body. This happens to all patients on bypass, all their tiny vessels leak and their tissues swell with fluid. This is usually rectified by giving them a diuretic to make them pee it off. Her face was so swollen, the admitting nurse could not even open her eyes to check her pupils. Hemodynamically (meaning her blood pressures and heart activity), she was very unstable. She continued to bleed through her chest tubes. She was still on ECMO on Sunday. In one thirty-hour period, she lost over eight times her normal blood volume, which was about 350 milliliters, the amount in a can of Coke. This means that something was bleeding somewhere. A post-op echocardiogram of her heart showed many problems, including the fact that her VSD repair was still leaking.

On Sunday, Dr. Odim decided to remove Jessica from ECMO. He wanted to do this in the PICU instead of taking her back to the OR because she was so very fragile. Normally one of two things would occur when a patient was removed from ECMO: either the patient would go to the OR, or the OR staff would come to the patient. Neither of these scenarios happened. No OR staff were called to PICU to assist even though they were literally steps away. Right down the hall. What followed was one of the most horrific events that I have ever heard of. To this day I wonder how this could have happened.

The PICU nurses were not prepared to remove this child from ECMO. They needed special cardiac instruments and sutures that were not available in their department. Again, these items were steps away in the OR. But even if they had gone looking, it would have been an almost impossible task to know what to look for and where to find it in an unfamiliar department. Even the PICU attending doctor stated that this procedure had never been successfully performed in the PICU. No one was in favour of doing this without the assistance of the OR staff. These concerns were discussed with Dr. Odim, who continued to insist that they would manage in the PICU and without OR staff. His arrogance was mind boggling.

Dave Smith the perfusionist was there, but the nurses from the OR on duty that day were not advised that this was happening. Dr. Odim did not call in the anesthetist either.

Taking out the cannulas like the ones that connected Jessica to the ECMO machine is a tricky business in a small child. Things can go wrong quickly … and they did. Jessica was losing a lot of blood prior to this procedure. When Dr. Odim removed the venous cannula from the right atrium of the heart, Jessica's blood pressure dropped dramatically as a massive amount of blood was lost. Dr. Odim made no announcement to let the perfusionist know he was removing the cannula. And he did not clamp the line before he removed it. Nor did he ask his assistant, Dr. Hancock, to do so. This is very important; everyone involved must be made aware of what is about to happen. A massive amount of blood was being lost around the cannula site and Dr. Odim could not stop it. He needed a special clamp and suture, neither of which was in the PICU. One of the PICU nurses ran to the OR to get them. In speaking to one of the OR nurses later, upon her arrival in the PICU, she described the situation as chaotic and scary. The OR nurses were unaware that this procedure was going on in the PICU until one of the nurses from the unit rushed in looking for equipment. They then ran over to see if they could help.

In the meantime, Dr. Odim attempted to pinch off the site (on this tiny heart which was the size of a plum) with his fingers. Jessica died before he could clamp or suture the tear. Her body was drained of blood. Even worse, it was discovered afterwards that the cannula—which should have been clamped to prevent blood from running out of it after it was removed—was left unclamped. So Jessica bled to death through both the unclamped cannula and the cannulation site. Since I wasn't present at that event, I was told of this disaster either that day or the next. When I spoke to Dave about it, he seemed so shocked and disturbed I was unable to get the full story from him. I don't think he had ever been in this kind of situation either.

I had never heard of such a disastrous event. Lots of things can go wrong, but any surgeon I had ever worked with made sure to check and double check everything before attempting such a dangerous procedure on such an unstable patient. It was unfathomable to me that Dr. Odim was so cavalier (a word I later heard another doctor use to describe him) about the situation. This was someone's child.

At autopsy, it was discovered that there was a needle near the bleeding site on the heart. Dr. Odim later stated that it was likely a needle from when he was trying to staunch the bleeding in PICU and not the missing needle from the surgical procedure. Either way, it was not considered a factor in her death. Also, the autopsy findings determined that neither of the two attempts at a patch repair of the VSD were properly done. It still leaked.

This was something that should have been taken to the head of the department of surgery, or the head of Children's Hospital right then and there. However, since I wasn't present at the time, I couldn't do or say anything. Perhaps there were discussions that I was not aware of at the time. If there were, they came to nothing.

I was so angry, sad, frightened, worried, confused; so many emotions were going through my mind. In my nursing career, I don't recall ever feeling more shocked—and I have seen some terrible things in my career. This feeling would become more prevalent as the year wore on. As a nurse, there seemed to be nothing I could do. I just could not understand how something like this could happen. And go unnoticed. Everyone I had previously worked with in the cardiac ORs, both adult and pediatric, had always been so careful, so thorough, so watchful, and so caring. No one ever took risks when a life was in jeopardy. Especially a child's life. They always made sure that all available equipment and staff were there. There were checks, doublechecks and triple checks. Things went wrong from time to time, but this was something entirely different.

Dr. Odim's big fingers trying to pinch off a bleeding hole in a baby's heart inside her tiny chest is an image I cannot erase from my mind. *What was he thinking?* To me this wasn't just a medical safety issue, it was a moral issue. *How could anyone put a helpless infant at risk?*

Jessica was the second child to die, and in speaking to some of the people involved, I concluded that the events leading to her death were disturbing to everyone, not just to me. It was totally outside of anyone's realm of experience. It wasn't going to be the last horrific thing I would see over the next few months.

CHAPTER 5

VINAY GOYAL

Vinay Goyal was a four-year-old boy, born on March 2, 1990 with multiple cardiac defects and Down Syndrome. He was adorable.

He was just a little guy with big dark eyes and black hair. He had a sweet nature but could be a bit of a fighter when he was frightened. He had several cardiac malformations including a VSD, a thickened wall of one of the chambers of his heart, an obstruction to the flow through one of his valves, and some underdeveloped anatomy within his heart, all of which impeded the flow of blood through it.

A BT shunt had been performed earlier in his life by Dr. Duncan. This shunt redirected the flow of blood through the heart and lungs and was left until he was old enough and big enough to have the actual repair done. In 1992, the first shunt was replaced with a larger one, again by Dr. Duncan. The plan was to do the definitive repair Vinay needed when he was a bit older.

As he grew, he began to have more and more blue spells and his exercise tolerance was decreasing. He needed the definitive repair. After Dr. Duncan left, plans to send Vinay out for the surgery, either to Saskatoon or Toronto, were discussed. The Goyal family was still undecided about where Vinay should go. In December 1993, they received news that a new surgeon had been hired and that Vinay could have his surgery in Winnipeg.

By early 1994, tests revealed that Vinay needed surgery sooner rather than later. He was at or near the top of the list for a surgical repair. His parents met Dr. Odim on March 1, 1994. During the discussions, Vinay's mother asked Dr. Odim if he had ever done this operation before. He assured her that he would not touch a child if he had not done the operation before. Was that an answer? He had seen several during his training, but had he performed one on his own? Not in our institution, so one could assume he hadn't, since this was his first job.

Vinay's surgery took place March 17. A complete repair of a double outlet right ventricle and Tetralogy of Fallot was performed. The next day, due to certain oxygen measurements within the heart, it was determined that the patch repair of the VSD was leaking. At that point, that was three out of three failed VSD repairs.

Vinay remained in the PICU for thirty-one days. He had a very difficult post-op course in PICU and was intubated and ventilated (a breathing tube and a machine assisting his breathing) most of the time he was there. The staff was concerned with his lack of progress. Normally, VSD repairs stayed in PICU two to four days.

The family was also very concerned. However, there seemed to be no option other than to stay the course. He was too sick to be transferred to another centre at that point.

A heart catheterization revealed that Vinay's problems had not been surgically solved and that there was no option other than another operation. This had been discussed with his parents and they felt that they had no choice but to go ahead. The option of sending Vinay out for this surgery was never presented to them. They called a friend who was a pediatric cardiologist in Toronto. He contacted Dr. Odim to discuss the case. As far as I know, nothing came of that conversation.

On April 18, Vinay was taken back to the OR to deal with the leaking VSD repair.

Just prior to the second operation, Dr. Jo Swartz, a cardiac anethetist, and Dr. Odim argued about replacing some of the monitoring lines.

Dr. Swartz, who like many anesthetists also worked in the PICU, had been involved in Vinay's care there and knew him well. She did not back down. At some point Dr. Odim remarked that she had a lot of testosterone. She ended the conversation at that point.

The entire operation was difficult and long. Leaks around the previous VSD repair were revealed and it was redone. I was the scrub nurse. It was physically and emotionally exhausting. We all knew Vinay. We had been following his progress in the PICU. I often wandered into the PICU to see him. I talked to the PICU nurses about him a couple of times. We were all worried. We wanted this to work for him.

Coming off bypass was rocky. Three events around this time occurred which surprised and disturbed all of us who were present in the OR. At one point, Dr. Odim asked for a syringe of adrenalin. I don't remember exactly why he did this, but after asking anesthesia to administer some adrenalin and not getting the result he wanted, he proceeded to dribble the adrenalin solution directly on the heart without alerting the anesthetist or her assistant. Immediately, the heart changed colour and contracted violently, creating dramatic changes in Vinay's blood pressure readings. When asked by Dr. Swartz for a reason for his actions, with the heart being so fragile and Vinay's hemodynamics being so unstable, instead of giving a medically based explanation, Dr. Odim asked if she preferred he throw the syringe on the floor.

The next event occurred when Dr. Odim requested a large syringe filled with saline. After I gave it to him, he used the heel of his had to forcefully squirt it against the new patch on the VSD, to "test it for leaks." This was also very disturbing for all of us, never having seen something like this before. He had just completed a repair on the VSD and now he was squirting saline under pressure against it. The tissues inside the heart were very delicate at that point and this pressure could potentially damage the new repair and the surrounding tissue. Again, it was shocking and disturbing to all of us. It confirmed my belief that Dr. Odim was rough and careless. I could not understand it.

Finally came the sudden decannulation of the aorta. When cannulating and decannulating during these operations, it is very important that everyone is aware of what is going on. Vinay was bleeding profusely and there was a disagreement as to the source. Was it surgical (such as a tear or rip in the tissues somewhere) or a coagulopathy (problems with clotting)? Dr. Swartz believed it was due to the former, while Dr. Odim believed the latter was the reason. When patients are bleeding a lot, blood products can be transfused directly into the patient through the aortic cannula by the perfusionist at the request of the anesthetist. It is the most direct and the fastest way to get the blood into the patient. Dr. Swartz asked Mike, the perfusionist, to do just that. However, Mike was unable to do so because a pump alarm went off alerting him that there was an obstruction: without informing anyone, Dr. Odim had clamped and removed the cannula. No one other than Dr. Odim and his assistant Dr. Hancock knew the line was out. Removal of all cannulas, and especially the aortic one, is ALWAYS announced and everyone must agree before it is removed. Mike seemed confused about what was happening. I was stunned and confused too. I didn't know what to do or say. I remember looking at Jo; she was as white as a sheet. This was totally outside my realm of experience. I looked back at Mike, who glanced at me as if to say *What is happening?* This event made it extremely difficult to transfuse Vinay. He desperately needed more blood. More importantly, there was still blood in the bypass machine (the pump) which could not be returned quickly to Vinay now. The aortic cannula is the last cannula to be removed and is always, in my experience, left in until everyone is sure that all the blood is returned and all potential sources of the bleeding are identified. That's just common sense. As it turned out, there was a tear in the heart that was bleeding profusely. Was that a result of the high-pressure irrigation of saline by the surgeon? Dr. Odim did not seem to know how that happened. There was no way to keep up with the blood loss now. Vinay quickly deteriorated and had a cardiac arrest. He was pronounced dead in the OR at 7:07 that evening. Dr. Odim later admitted that taking out the aortic cannula contributed to Vinay's death.

As we were clearing up the operating field after the surgery, I paused and stood over Vinay, looking at this tiny little guy. So frail and fragile looking, but he had been such a fighter.

Jo Swartz came around to the side of the OR table and stood beside me. She picked up his hand and held it for a minute. She looked at him and then at me and said, "He was my friend." They had spent a lot of time together in PICU.

Later, after we had bathed Vinay, we decided to have his parents view him in the post-anesthesia care unit, or recovery room as it is commonly called. It was away from the hustle and bustle of the PICU and would afford the family some privacy. It was late in the evening by then and no one was there. We dimmed the lights and advised PICU that he'd be there soon and they could bring the family in to see him. As Carol Dupuis wheeled him down the hall, his teddy bear fell off the stretcher. It was on a shelf underneath him. She picked it up and tucked it in beside him. As she walked away, she wept.

None of us will forget him.

VINAY WAS THE THIRD CHILD to have a VSD repair and the third child to die. All three repairs leaked and failed. Gary Caribou and Jessica Ulimaumi preceded him. That was three out of three.

My question was how many red flags needed to waved before someone noticed?

Why was no one paying attention by then? Who was in charge of this new surgeon? No one seemed to know.

Watching Dr. Odim, I was disturbed by how rough he was and how he handled these tiny hearts. This was very upsetting and disturbing to all of us. Not just because of the way things had gone wrong in Vinay's operation, but what had happened to Gary and Jessica prior to this. These ongoing problems with cannulation, bleeding, long bypass times, and lengthy stays in PICU. There were issues with the kids that survived that were becoming more and more worrisome. Several had severe complications. Failure of the repairs, excessive bleeding, and returning to the OR became the common threads. It was starting to add up, and not in a good way.

The term, "learning curve" was mentioned several times. I didn't get it. Several people seemed to think that I should have accepted the fact that Dr. Odim was on a learning curve insofar as his patient outcomes were concerned. Give the guy a chance, was the refrain. But I knew what a learning curve meant. To me, it meant starting with simpler things and working your way up to the more difficult cases. Perhaps an analogy could be made by learning to play a musical instrument. A pianist doesn't start with a Sonata. They start with very simple pieces and after much practicing and studying, progress to more and more difficult ones. When a new surgeon starts operating, it surely does not make sense to take on a complex procedure, thereby putting a patient's life at risk. Who among us would want our child to be part of this kind of a learning curve? Most surgeons get their feet wet with simpler cases. Their patients survive. Bad things happen from time to time, but surgeons want their patients to do well. They don't take risks when it involves someone's life. Besides, it makes their stats look bad.

In the PICU, Donna Feser, the nurse manager, was worried too. They had asked Dr. Odim for help in putting together a cardiac bin with some special supplies to have at the ready in the unit. These items would include sutures, special pacemaker equipment, perhaps some sterile instruments that would be ready in case a child's chest needed to be reopened in the PICU. This had happened in the past and would prove to be very important later in the cases of Alyssa Still and others. If a cardiac patient deteriorated in the PICU, things happened very quickly. It was unlikely that the OR staff would still be in the OR in the middle of the night. If they were, it was because they were dealing with another emergency and might not be able to help. So the PICU staff would be on their own, at least until we got there, if we were called. This is one reason having a cardiac bin was so important. There was no time to run around trying to find things in the OR, particularly if you didn't know what you were looking for.

These two groups of nurses, OR and PICU, were very competent and highly trained in their own fields. *They were not interchangeable.* This was something that most doctors knew, but I always felt that Dr. Odim did not understand that concept. It seemed to me that to him a nurse was a nurse was a nurse. To my knowledge, he never assisted the nurses, and

I was asked on a couple of occasions to help with this cardiac bin project. Having my own difficulties with Dr. Odim's lack of response to my requests, I understood their frustration and I was glad to help.

Nurses are given a lot of responsibility but very little power. It is expected that our concerns be limited to our professional duties and that we not critique those "above" us. In days gone by, nurses were told to stand by and be silent. This was due to the old-fashioned notion that nurses are to be subservient to the doctor. The fact that nurses wore caps years ago is a throwback to female servants wearing little hats or some sort of head covering. Gender equality has come a long way even since I graduated from nursing school in 1969, but we are still not at the end of that fight. Back then doctors were usually men, nurses were women. Nowadays, more and more men are getting their nursing degrees and medical schools are graduating more and more women. But the gender and hierarchy issues are still there. The fact that Dr. Odim told a female anesthetist that she had a lot of testosterone when she disagreed with him is a clear example that the problem still exists. It illustrated perfectly how the breakdown of communication and trust within the team happens.

I KNEW HEAD OF PEDIATRIC SURGERY, Dr. Nathan Wiseman, well and I felt I could approach him. On more than one occasion I asked him to come into the OR and see what was going on. Apart from the odd quick peek, he never observed a procedure start to finish. At one point when I think he was frustrated with my persistent requests and comments, he told me that he "didn't take orders from nurses." Later he would explain his reasons. He said that his presence in the OR with Dr. Odim would change the dynamic in the room and therefore he would not really get a reliable indication of the problems. Once I heard that I still felt unhappy, but I could understand his reasoning.

One of the biggest lessons I learned during this time was that although I knew I was a highly regarded and competent OR nurse, I was still seen as overstepping when I voiced my concerns to physicians and hospital authorities. Despite my twenty-five years of nursing experience, with more than twenty in the OR, much of it in cardiac and trauma surgery, my concerns were generally dismissed by the physicians, as were those of the other nurses, so we decided to go through more official channels.

I was not alone in my concerns. Irene, the anesthesia nurse, was also worried. Another nurse in the OR, Carol Dupuis, who frequently worked in the cardiac OR with me, was also voicing her concerns. She and I had several conversations and all of us went to Karin Dixon, our nurse manager, and later, to her boss, Isobel Boyle, the director of nursing for the Children's Centre at the time. They listened to our concerns and took them further. They had conversations with Dr. Wiseman, and with Dr. Agnes Bishop and Dr. Brian Postl who were the heads of the department of pediatrics. (Dr. Bishop left that year and Dr. Postl took over.)

Irene and I met with Isobel Boyle more than once that April to voice our concerns, and after Vinay died, we were back in her office again. It wasn't just about Vinay; it was about all Dr. Odim's patients who had come through the OR. So many issues and complications, so many tense moments in the OR. Poor communication. Scrambling to stop unexpected bleeding, getting on and off bypass safely, all the smaller mishaps we witnessed. We hadn't experienced anything like this. None of us felt comfortable doing even the simplest cases. In the past, I had scrubbed alone for most cardiac cases. I no longer felt safe doing that. I let Karin know that she should assign two scrub nurses for Dr. Odim's cases from now on. When things went wrong, a second pair of hands made a big difference.

The nurses in the PICU and NICU were raising concerns with Irene, who was in and out of their units on a regular basis. They worried about excessive bleeding post-operatively and procedures normally requiring a trip to the OR, such as reopening and closure of patients' chests, being performed in the units. Isobel arranged for people from the hospital's critical incident response team to come over and meet with us to help us deal with the stress and grief.

Around this time, Irene and I had a discussion that later turned out to be pivotal. She told me that I should start taking notes, at home on my own computer, documenting what was happening. Irene wasn't the only friend who suggested I do this. So far, Gary, Jessica, and Vinay were children of visible minority parents. Gary and Jessica were from remote northern communities. Vinay's parents were from South Asia. Their first language was not English. They did not have an "in" with the medical community or maybe even a clear understanding of what had happened to their child. Someday, Irene said, someone with an "in" was going to know that this shouldn't have happened. They would be asking questions and perhaps a lawsuit will be the result. She was thinking ahead, and since I was there all the time and would likely be called as a witness, she thought I should make my own personal notes. I agreed, and after that, I started to make notes at home, at night or the following morning. I was documenting what had happened in my own words. Carol Dupuis began to make notes as well. So, on several evenings, late into the night, I sat at my PC at home typing and crying. Reading those notes now still affects me so deeply that I avoid it. I rarely look at them. These notes became of great interest later.

One problem seemed to be the undying loyalty of Dr. Odim's assistant in the OR, Dr. B.J. Hancock. She was also a new surgeon, just starting out her practice in pediatric general surgery. She had recently completed her training in Montreal. One of her duties was to be Dr. Odim's dedicated assistant. One of Dr. Duncan's complaints when he left Winnipeg was that he did not have one. Most cardiac surgeons have someone who assists them regularly. Things obviously go more smoothly when your assistant knows you. This was part of Dr. Hancock's job now that she was on staff. It seemed that she supported Dr. Odim unconditionally. None of us could understand it. Later, when there were other surgical disasters, she would always be in line with his version of events. Even when four or five people described an incident, the two of them would often state that they didn't recall it. There could be documentation on the anesthetist's, nurse's, and the perfusionist's records about the event but often they both said they didn't recall it happening.

It blew my mind. Doctors stick together, but this was beyond the pale. People seeing any event often have differing memories of how it went down. That's a well-known phenomenon. This didn't seem to be what was happening here. It often came down to Dr. Odim's and Dr. Hancock's recollections, or lack thereof, versus the recollections of several other members of the team and the computer-generated documentation from the monitors, which don't lie. This is the only time I ever experienced this.

Where was this going? I began to feel Dr. Odim's animosity toward me and other female members of the team more and more. *Did I have too much of a smart mouth? Was I talking too much? Was I disrespectful in his eyes? Did I make him nervous?* I spoke up when necessary and the anesthetists and perfusionists often spoke to me during the cases. I had been told by other nurses that I was scary sometimes... (much to my surprise). *Was all this my fault?* I tried to keep things going smoothly, keep the noise level (the "din" as Dr. Odim called it) down, reduce the amount to chatter to what was absolutely necessary. I kept hoping that things were going to turn around and improve.

Then, two days after Vinay, there was Daniel Terziski.

CHAPTER 6

DANIEL TERZISKI

Daniel was born in Winnipeg on March 18, 1994. He went home from the hospital with his mother a few days later. Not long after, Daniel started to develop problems. He seemed weak, tired easily and had difficulty feeding. His mother took him to see his pediatrician. She was told to supplement his feedings. A few days later, he was taken to another pediatrician in the same group who, upon assessing the baby, told his mother to take him to Children's Hospital right away. Daniel was admitted to the NICU that day.

He was diagnosed as having tricuspid atresia (an undeveloped valve on the right side of his heart, or, in Daniel's case, an absent valve). He also had what is known as a Transposition of the Great Arteries, the great arteries being the aorta and the pulmonary artery. In a normal heart, the aorta, which takes blood to the body, arises from the left ventricle, and the pulmonary artery, which takes blood to the lungs, arises from the right ventricle. In a Transposition of the Great Arteries, the aorta and the pulmonary arteries are reversed, aorta on the right, pulmonary artery on the left. There was a small VSD, an undeveloped (rudimentary) right ventricle, and narrowed aortic arch. Essentially Daniel had only one ventricle.

According to his medical records, a fetal assessment at six months gestation showed a normal fetus with no cardiac defects. This assessment was questioned later and there were further discussions with the radiologist as to how this significant defect was missed. Often when a serious malformation or defect is detected by a fetal assessment, usually by an ultrasound, and it is known that surgery is going to be required shortly after birth, arrangements can be made for the mother to give birth in a city where they can access the expertise necessary. Like an expert surgeon. If that is not something that the family wants, or the doctors feel that there is time, a team can be readied to fly the baby to another centre soon after its birth. So fetal assessments are critical and could have been helpful in Daniel's case.

Daniel's heart defects were considered extremely serious and life threatening. Daniel would require a "Modified Norwood" operation very soon in order to survive (STAT 5). This surgery was developed by a Dr. Norwood in the United States in the mid-1980s. The idea was to create a new "aorta" attached to the pulmonary artery. A small passageway was created to regulate the blood to the lungs as well.

The Modified Norwood is considered one of the most difficult and complex heart operations performed on babies. However, without the operation or a heart transplant, one hundred percent of children with Transposition of the Great Arteries would die within days or weeks. Usually, these children had essentially a single working ventricle doing the job of two ventricles and their life-expectancy was short. The Modified Norwood is the first of a multi-stage repair (usually three stages), something that would buy some time and give the heart a chance to grow. Then there would be another operation later, when the child was about six months of age, and if that went well, another at about two years of age. Even in the best hands, the first procedure was very risky. Later, at the inquest, it was determined that taking on a case like this at this point was unwise. In 1994, this procedure was rarely performed even in large, established heart centres. Three of our recent VSD patients had died, and all had been STAT 2 or 3. Why were we attempting this?

Daniel was becoming very ill and too unstable to transfer out to another centre. Daniel's parents were consulted, and they had several conversations with Dr. Giddins and Dr. Odim. At one point, Daniel's mother asked if a cardiac surgeon who was of the same Bulgarian descent as them could be brought to Winnipeg from Montreal to operate on Daniel. They were told that there were legal and licensing issues with bringing in a surgeon from another province. According to the parents, Dr. Giddins became quite defensive during this discussion. The parents then asked about transferring Daniel to Montreal for his surgery. They were told that the Winnipeg team was capable of performing this surgery. Dr. Odim's notes stated that all options were discussed, including palliation, transplantation (which was not an option in Winnipeg), and the Norwood repair. The parents had opted for the last option, according to him. He did not mention the discussions around having the surgeon come to Winnipeg or having Daniel transferred to another centre. The family stated that they were dissuaded from those options.

Daniel was in the hospital for several days before his surgery and had deteriorated considerably. He certainly was not in optimal shape when he went to the OR on April 20. This was the first time one of Dr. Odim's patients would be going to the NICU post-op.

There were two different ICUs at Children's. The Pediatric Intensive Care Unit (PICU) cared for all critically ill children up to about sixteen to eighteen years of age. They did care for infants, but they were usually several months old. The NICU cared for newborns (under 30 days of age), or neonates, as they were called. These babies usually came directly from the labour floor and were often preemies, never having left the hospital. Occasionally, like Daniel, they were admitted from home. They were very young, mostly a few days or a week old, and had developed some issue that required hospital intensive care.

Prior to the date of surgery, Deb Armitage, one of the NICU's senior nurses; the NICU attending doctor; and Dr. Odim sat down to discuss Daniel's post-op care. Deb ran into the same problem the PICU nurses and I had with Dr. Odim. No specific answers, always vague and repeating his mantra, "Whatever you are used to will be fine." Deb went a bit further, telling me that a light bulb went off over her head when, it seemed to her, Dr. Odim did not know what he needed or wanted post-op. He had no idea. In Deb's experience, the surgeons were very clear in their orders as to the monitoring and the care of their patients in the NICU following surgery. This had been the experience of all of us who worked with cardiac patients. The same problems arose again and again. Communication with his team was not Dr. Odim's forte and it is so important when creating care plans and protocols for patients. Everyone must be on the same page and know what to expect, what drugs, equipment and interventions are necessary. All contingencies must be considered and planned for.

Given the problems at the time, I was shocked when I heard that we were going to be doing a Norwood. *Why were we running before we could walk? What was the thinking behind this decision?* Despite my misgivings, I approached Dr. Odim about whether there was anything special we needed for this case. Again, I received no information. I asked about one specific set of instruments that our OR did not have but that I could borrow from the adult OR in our centre. This was something that I noted Dr. Duncan had used. Dr. Odim told me that I needn't get this set of instruments. I did anyway, and he asked for them during the surgery. Again, did he really know what he needed? It didn't seem so to me. Was I supposed to figure this all out for him? Not in my job description. But I did it anyway and was thankful that I had those instruments there that day.

Daniel's operation took over ten hours. There were a lot of difficulties. Dr. Odim constructed a shunt at one point to redirect the blood in the heart. When Daniel came off bypass it was determined that the shunt was too small. Dr. Odim had to redo it. Twice. Each time Daniel was put back on bypass. These events increased Daniel's time on bypass considerably.

He came back to the NICU in a very critical condition. Dr. Odim had opted not to close his chest and Daniel came back with silastic sheeting over it. The baby was extremely fragile. About forty minutes after he arrived, his oxygen levels fell and Dr. Odim decided to go into Daniel's chest right then in the NICU. This caused a great deal of consternation among the staff. They were not prepared for this. They had asked for guidance from Dr. Odim at the pre-operative meeting and had the usual lack of response from him. Small procedures were done in the NICU from time to time, but nothing like this. Someone ran down one floor to the OR to see if one of the cardiac nurses was around and to get some equipment. I was thankful that I was still in the OR, cleaning up after Daniel's surgery, and was able to collect some items to take up to NICU and assist in the resuscitation.

Any nurse in the OR would have been able to help; there was a tray of sterile cardiac instruments always at the ready. I collected what I needed as fast as I could and went up to the unit. When I got there the scene was chaotic. No one seemed to know what to do. They seemed unprepared for such a sick baby, something the staff had tried to anticipate by sitting down with Dr. Odim prior to the operation. Dr. Odim wanted Heparin drawn up. This was for a tiny baby, and, not being an NICU nurse, I didn't know the precise dosage. I asked him, and he didn't know either. Dosages on small infants are calculated precisely based on the child's weight and body surface area. I barely remember the next few minutes.

I wanted to stand back and let the doctors do their thing, but it seemed like I was drawn into the fray. The pacemaker needed to be adjusted. I think Dr. Reimer, the anesthetist, figured that out, since Dr. Odim and Dr. Giddins did not seem to understand how to set the external pacer. I remember feeling terrified and helpless. I was fighting down panic the entire time. I tried to remain calm. But this wasn't my area of expertise. I could help with the operative side of things, but calculating medications by weight or body surface area and adjusting pacemakers to counteract dysrhythmias was done by either the doctors or NICU nurses, who had the specialized expertise. Just as those nurses in the NICU did not feel they could assist in reopening the chest of an infant who had undergone major surgery, I was not comfortable doing their job. Because of my inability to fully assist in the resuscitation even though I was highly trained in my specialty, I had to listen to Dr. Odim's disparaging remarks throughout this event. Laying blame where it wasn't warranted.

Despite about forty minutes of desperate resuscitation efforts, Daniel passed away at 8:59 p.m. We were all devastated. I think we all believed that had Daniel been transferred to a bigger centre with an experienced surgeon, he would have had a better chance. He had no chance with Dr. Odim, in my opinion. Zero. The experience and skill just wasn't there yet, especially for a complex and relatively new procedure like this one. During his training, Dr. Odim would have been allowed to do more and more in the OR as his skills developed. First it would be opening the chest and helping with the cannulation process, then later performing a cannulation himself under the guidance of the surgeon. He would watch the repairs and likely be allowed to do a simple procedure, again under the watchful eye of the staff surgeon. He would be allowed to close the chest. If all went well, he would go on to more complex cases. I doubt that Dr. Odim had ever done an entire operation on his own while he was training. I don't think any cardiac surgeon would have felt comfortable to let a resident do it all without supervision. As a fully qualified surgeon, certainly he could go ahead and do whatever he wanted, but most surgeons not only care about their patients but they also worry about their own morbidity and mortality numbers. In the name of caution and prudence, surely most fledgling surgeons would start with simpler cases, hone their skills and if all went well, move on to the more complex operations as they came along. Winnipeg had been sending out critically ill children during the months we had no surgeon. Admittedly, this was costly, but I don't think cost would have been a factor in the decision-making process, especially early on. Patient safety was certainly paramount.

Sometime later, Dr. Giddins stated that this case improved his assessment of the surgical team because Daniel made it out of the OR when so many children who had this particular operation did not. But Daniel had died about an hour later, so how did that make sense? Kids with this type of very complex congenital heart defect are extremely high risk and will die without surgical intervention. I am not a mind reader, so I don't know what motivated him to say something like that. It seems he never thought Daniel would make it as far as he did. Certainly, if that was the case, why operate at all?

Several years later, Daniel's mother approached me at a restaurant. It was a popular hamburger place outside the city, with kind of a retro vibe, red vinyl booths and chrome tables and chairs. It was on the Red River and in the summer, people pulled up in their vintage cars and motorcycles and put their food orders in. They sat on picnic tables along the riverbank or walked around admiring the vehicles on display. I was standing at the ice cream counter with my teenage son and his girlfriend putting in our order. Danica Terziski came up to me. I didn't recognize her at first, although I knew I'd seen her somewhere. I tried to figure out who she was. I always hate it when people recognize me and I don't know who they are. I am notoriously terrible at remembering names. She introduced herself, we spoke, and she hugged and thanked me for what I and the other nurses had done. She said she was grateful for everything that the nurses had tried to do. I was somewhat overcome, and I certainly didn't want to break down in this crowded restaurant on a Sunday afternoon. I was unable to think or speak at first. It was a very emotional moment. I told her I was so sorry. It was a brief conversation. She was lovely. My son was standing nearby, watching this exchange. As we drove home, all he said was "That was intense, Mom."

Some of the pain I had been feeling fell away that day. I am never really aware of the amount of pain I carry with me because of what happened in 1994. It's apparently buried deep in my subconscious. It resurfaces with a vengeance when I am asked to speak about what happened, so most of the time I avoid talking about any of it. However, I recognize it when something positive happens, like the incident I just described. It's like a bit of it falls away and some healing occurs. For these moments, I am grateful.

CHAPTER 7

ALYSSA STILL

Alyssa was a beautiful four-month-old child. Cute, chubby, with big eyes and dark hair that stood up all over her head. A very pretty little baby girl. I still have a lovely photo of her. She was born in Thunder Bay, Ontario and when she was diagnosed with Tetralogy of Fallot, her mother, Donna, opted to have her seen in Winnipeg rather than Toronto or London, Ontario because it was closer to home.

Tetralogy of Fallot is a group of defects which in Alyssa's case consisted of mild biventricular hypertrophy (thickened heart muscle), a VSD, and a mild right ventricular outflow tract obstruction. Her pulmonary arteries were narrowed as well. When she arrived at Children's Hospital, there were also some concerns regarding her lungs. Other tests indicated that Alyssa was otherwise a healthy baby and a good candidate for a repair, which was usually done at around six months of age.

A few days before her scheduled surgery in April, Alyssa had a cold and was put on antibiotics for a week. Her surgery was postponed. She was readmitted when she recovered. On May 2, a chest X-ray was done. Dr. Odim wrote on her chart that he felt that she had recovered sufficiently for them to go ahead with her surgery as long as a swab for

RSV (respiratory syncytial virus) was negative. However, the radiologist, Dr. Martin Reed, stated in his report that her right lung showed some signs of pneumonia. This report was made available on Alyssa's chart the day before her surgery, but it appears neither Dr. Odim nor Dr. Giddins read it. Alyssa's family was also not made aware of this issue.

Her surgery took place on May 5. Dr. Odim patched the VSD with a Dacron Patch, dilated the pulmonary arteries and pulmonary valve and excised the right ventricular muscle bundle in order to allow for better blood flow through the heart. The bypass time was long.

On arrival at the PICU, Alyssa was stable, according to Dr. Odim. She showed symptoms of fluid overload, meaning she had extra fluid in her body, which was verycommon in patients who had been on bypass during surgery. Fluid intake and output is closely monitored by perfusionists, anesthesia, and nurses during surgery. IVs and blood products are run in during the operation and urine output is precisely measured. Sometimes there is either a positive or negative fluid balance. A positive fluid balance is usually resolved with medication to get rid of the excess fluid.

Alyssa was puffy and her blood pressure was a bit low. This isn't that unusual following bypass surgery, so during the evening, she was started on a medication to support her blood pressure and a diuretic to make her pee off some of the excess fluid. At around 1 a.m., Alyssa's nurse, Colleen Kiesman, noticed that she had a cough when she was suctioned. She was still intubated, and now and then a small amount of secretions would collect and need to be suctioned away. At around 3:45 a.m., Colleen suctioned her again. This time there were some thick blood-tinged secretions. At this point, Alyssa's blood pressure and heart rate began to drop. All children who have open heart surgery go to the PICU with a temporary pacemaker in place. It is not turned on unless it is needed. At this time, Colleen turned on the pacemaker, but there was no capture, the heart rate did not increase as expected. This made Colleen and the attending doctor who was now at the bedside wonder if the leads had been positioned on the heart correctly during surgery. Dr. Odim was called and he reopened the chest. He asked for the internal defibrillator paddles and another set of epicardial pacing wires since the ones he had placed on Alyssa's heart were not functioning properly. These had to come from the OR. At around 4:00 a.m., I was awakened at home by a call from a PICU nurse who asked me where these items were kept in the OR. I had to direct her to the right theatre and correct cupboard over the phone.

A resuscitation was begun but Alyssa's heart rate never recovered. At 5:02 a.m., Alyssa died. Following the attempted resuscitation, Dr. Odim told Colleen that it was likely the suctioning that caused Alyssa to have what is called a vaso-vagal response and subsequent arrest. Was he blaming her? This was extremely distressing and traumatizing for her to hear. The PICU attending doctor, Dr. Murray Kesselman, heard this exchange and disagreed with Dr. Odim's statement. He told Colleen that he likely would have done the same thing. Later, the autopsy results disproved Dr. Odim's statement as well.

I was back at work that morning. When I had received the call from the PICU nurse asking for help, I had assumed that a different child was in trouble. The child I was thinking of was also a patient of Dr. Odim and had been in the PICU since April 13. We had heard that this child was having a rocky post-operative course. It never occurred to me that it was Alyssa that prompted the call. We were all so happy when she came out of the OR and seemed to be doing well. I remember thinking that perhaps we had finally turned a corner. She had been transferred to PICU in stable condition. We all felt good about Alyssa when we went home that day.

As I walked into the OR that morning, I was met by Dr. Swartz, who informed me that Alyssa had died. We went into the break room for a few minutes, and I just sat there barely able to speak. I could NOT believe it. It was a shock. I felt such disappointment and grief. We all felt it. It was totally demoralizing. I was sitting in the OR staff lounge crying when Irene came in and sat with me for a while. We were both devastated. Neither of us knew what to do. After Gary, Jessica, Vinay, and Daniel, all in a few short weeks, this was a terrible blow. Kids with Tetralogy of Fallot were tricky to treat, but most did well post-operatively, in our experience.

The autopsy report was disturbing. There was a suture on the coronary sinus, which drains blood from the heart muscle itself into the right atrium and is part of the heart's normal anatomy. Did this suture close the sinus? Why was it there? An obstruction of blood flow through the coronary sinus could cause edema or congestion and dysfunction of the heart muscle. Could it have caused Alyssa's death? A leak in the VSD repair was found (again).

Another troubling thing was the lack of response when the pacemaker was activated. It should have increased the heart rate right away. Pacemaker wires, which are about twenty-four inches long, are attached with tiny hooks onto the surface of the heart at the end of the procedure just before the surgeon begins to close the chest. The wires come out of the chest and are then ready to be attached to a pacemaker device, a small gadget about the size of a remote control, with several dials and buttons on it. All these children had them post-operatively. Sometimes the kids didn't need to be paced and the pacemaker was never turned on. They were there, just in case. The wires could be easily pulled out through the skin when they were no longer needed.

The PICU attending doctor, Dr. Kesselman, had been concerned about the pacemaker wires because recently there had been situations where they had not worked properly on some of Dr. Odim's other post-op cardiac patients. I was tasked with contacting the company that manufactured them to let them know we had a problem, as well as having them examined by someone in the biomedical department at the hospital. Not long after Alyssa's death, I went into the PICU to talk to Dr. Kesselman about the pacing wires. I had heard from the biomedical department at the hospital after they had tested them to make sure they functioned properly. The wires were fine, there was nothing defective about them. I approached Dr. Kesselman, who was standing at the foot of a patient's bed watching the monitor. I told him that the wires we were using seemed to be fine. Keeping his eyes on the monitor, the doctor said, "The wires aren't the problem." Nothing else was said. I got the point and I walked away.

All these factors were troubling, especially when Dr. Odim seemed to want to pin the blame on the nurse.

I WAS BECOMING more and more distressed. What was going on? Like everyone else, I had been star-struck by Dr. Odim's qualifications. I still couldn't get my head around the fact that he didn't seem to know what he was doing. We had all been led to believe that he was highly trained and qualified. Was there some kind of misunderstanding? There were times as I was watching him when I thought that he wasn't qualified to be doing these types of cases. And why was Dr. Giddins selecting and referring patients that were obviously above this surgeon's level of skill? These were supposed to be intelligent men. *And why was nobody watching and monitoring the restart of this program? Who was in charge?* These were questions that plagued my mind that year. I didn't want to criticize anyone. I just wanted to come in and do my job and feel good about it at the end of the day. I wanted to take good care of my patients. It seemed that there were so many unanswered questions and concerns that were not being addressed.

I was scared. I didn't know at that time that things were about to change.

PART TWO
SECOND THOUGHTS

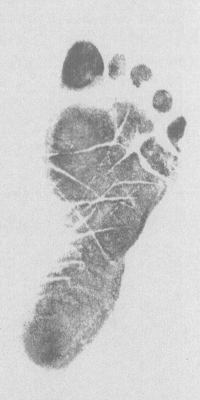

THE ANESTHETISTS SAY "NO"

Things were not going well. Intra-op and post-op bleeding was continuing to be a problem. Communication was poor. Animosity between the different members of the team was getting worse. Concerns were raised again when another child encountered excessive bleeding problems after surgery. This child was taken back to the OR the day after his surgery due to issues with the shunt Dr. Odim had constructed. He could not maintain his oxygen levels. Again, there were differences of opinion regarding the cause of the bleeding. As the second procedure was finishing up, Dr. Hancock pointed out some bleeding sites that needed attention. Again, Dr. Odim seemed to assume that the bleeding was due to a clotting problem and not something he'd done. He seemed to want that to be true. It was as if he didn't want to bother looking for the source of the bleeding. Too much trouble?

Sometimes I thought he simply enjoyed the status of being a heart surgeon, walking around the hospital with his white lab coat, his name embroidered on the pocket, over his fancy shirts and bowties. Maybe he didn't really want to do all the hard work. Taking the time to look for a bleeder wasn't glamorous. It was tedious and time consuming. This time, Dr. Hancock insisted that they look at these sites and deal with the issue.

There were several concerns raised around this time by the PICU regarding excessive bleeding. Gary Caribou had lost 200 cc during the first hour he was in the PICU. Jessica Ulimaumi lost over 600 cc in her first twenty-four hours in the PICU. It is difficult to keep up with that kind of blood loss. The acceptable amount of blood loss in a small child is around 10 cc per kilogram of body weight per hour, and if that continues for two hours, return to the OR is usually warranted.

In any team, there is the leader, and if there is a good leader, the team feels they can come to that person with their ideas and concerns. Everyone wants to work together to make things run smoothly and efficiently. It doesn't matter what the job is. In our case, we wanted the children to do well. We knew that not all of them would. That was the reality of the type of work we did. However, this situation was different. Children who had VSDs for example, generally had done well in the past, but now we had lost all three out of the three patients Dr. Odim had operated on. We needed to figure out why.

At some point in time, I think many of us nurses and anesthetists had come to the conclusion that it was difficult to discuss our concerns with Dr. Odim. Dr. Giddins seemed to think that there was no problem. To me, Dr. Odim seemed unapproachable. Up to that point, he had been polite but dismissive. The usual mantra, "whatever you have will be fine," had been replaced with snide comments and criticisms, sometimes said with a smirk and a hidden accusation.

A few months before Dr. Odim arrived, while I was away on vacation, some human tissue (homografts) that were kept in a tank of liquid nitrogen were ruined. I was responsible for making sure this tank was always full of liquid nitrogen to keep these homografts frozen. The tank had an audible alarm which alerted us when it was getting low. I checked it every couple of days. When the levels got low, I ordered a new tank. When I went on vacation, I assigned this duty to another nurse. When I returned to work, I checked the tank and it was dry. The homografts, worth about $30,000, were destroyed. I was horrified. I spoke to Karin Dixon and explained that I had left this in the hands of another nurse and that he had failed to check the tank. He denied this, but Karin had been aware of the backup plan, so she knew this wasn't my fault. But just the same, I felt terrible. Dr. Odim had been made aware of what had happened and on more than one occasion he brought it up, often with a smirk, asking me how it was possible this happened. The insinuation seemed clear; it was my fault ... even though I had been on vacation.

As well, on several occasions, he commented on the fact that I was working part-time. I worked four days per week with a lot of overtime, which often added up to more than full-time hours in the end. It was as if he was questioning my commitment to the job. These snide comments ate away at my morale. All I could do was try to smile and walk away. He was a guy who liked to twist the knife. Perhaps he was hoping I'd get fed up and walk away completely.

ON MAY 16, the hospital's section of pediatric anesthesia had a meeting. Because of the concerns with the morbidity and mortality with the cases to date, Dr. Swartz, Dr. McNeill, Dr. Wong, and Dr. Reimer made the decision to withdraw their services, effective the next day, May 17. They specified that they would no longer give anesthetics to children having open cases on CP Bypass. Their section head, Dr. Douglas Craig, was present at this meeting and supported the decision. It was a dramatic move, one that would essentially shut down the pediatric cardiac program. They sent a memo to Dr. Wiseman, the head of pediatric surgery, to alert everyone. It was copied to Dr. Craig and Dr. Blanchard, department heads of anesthesia and surgery respectively.

There was definitely some blow-back to the anesthetists' decision. Dr. Blanchard was astounded. He wondered why the medical members of the team hadn't worked out their problems before getting to this point. Dr. Bishop, head of the pediatric department, was angry that she had not been forewarned prior to the slowdown. One of her concerns had to do with what would happen to the patients who had been booked for surgery in the following days and weeks.

Dr. Giddins testified later that he was unaware of any problems between the anesthetists and Dr. Odim. Curious comment because surely he had spent enough time in the OR to witness some friction. Dr. Odim was also surprised at the anesthetists' action. He attributed any friction to personality differences. He felt that concerns should have been discussed in the last Morbidity and Mortality Rounds. Most of us didn't feel comfortable announcing our concerns in that environment. There were medical students and other people who were there for teaching purposes or were loosely connected to the program and perhaps shouldn't be involved in these discussions or even be made aware of the program's difficulties.

But the bottom line was that children had died, and the hospital's anesthetists had essentially shut down the program. As a result, the Paediatric Cardiac Review Team was formed to review the program to date. Dr. Wiseman was to lead it, and henceforth it was known as the Wiseman Committee.

CHAPTER 9

THE WISEMAN COMMITTEE

I was the only nurse named to the Wiseman Committee. I was not sure why. Where were the other nurses who had worked with me in the OR and the ones who worked in the Variety Heart Centre, PICU, and NICU? They certainly had things to say. We were definitely underrepresented. Some of the nurses from those departments inquired as to whether they could be part of the committee and were told there was no reason for them to attend. Another problem was that it was unclear who I was to report to. No one ever said anything about that. However, I was soon made to feel that my concerns weren't really important anyway, and that I should not share what was said in the meetings with anyone. I was a token.

On one occasion, a seemingly angry Dr. Giddins marched into the meeting. He was a tall thin man in his forties. He reminded me of Ichabod Crane. He had a temper; I had heard about it and witnessed it in the past. He told the committee that he had been approached by a pediatrician who asked him what was going on with the program. Should she stop referring patients for surgery? He wondered how she knew that the program had problems. He seemed angry about that, and I felt at that point that anything we discussed at these meetings was not supposed to leave the room. I felt intimidated and wondered if he thought that I was the "guilty party."

The first meeting was held on May 18, 1994. To me the whole thing was a waste of time. Not once was the issue of surgical competence addressed. By anyone. Ever. Apparently, Dr. Wiseman had already decided that it wasn't an issue. It was all about personality differences. And he ran the meetings. He seemed to believe that the nurses and anesthetists were the problem. Later I learned that the people to whom he reported had been told this.

Surgeons can be arrogant. I knew that at the time. A lot of them had a lousy bedside manner, and were, in fact, technicians who didn't really take a holistic view of their patients. It was all about the problem. I was okay with that as long as they did good work. Years ago, people would ask me for advice in finding a good doctor/surgeon. I would often tell them not to be surprised if the one I recommended seemed to be a bit of a jerk. A lot of them were, but they were very good at what they did.

Dr. Wiseman was not like that. He had always been friendly and approachable. He always seemed to know about his patients and their families, and although he sometimes got angry and had outbursts in the OR, I had considered him an ally and friend. He had written a funny letter to me when I had moved away to Regina for a few years. He filled me in with all the OR goings on since I had left.

I knew that on some level he believed me, that he didn't think I was making things up. But, bottom line… I was still "just a nurse." He seemed to be siding with his colleague, another surgeon, and by doing this he let me down.

One thing I have always said is that people hardly ever surprise me, but they almost always disappoint me. This was certainly the case with Dr. Wiseman. I wasn't really surprised, but I certainly was disappointed.

We had several meetings. Nothing was resolved in the end.

Dr. Wiseman rarely took notes or minutes. Later, Dr. Ullyot from anethesia said that when he did take minutes or notes, they were always late, or they never came at all, and they were never read or signed off at the subsequent meetings.

At the first meeting the guidelines for the review were set out. They included, among other things, discussions about the program results to date, the need for a way to express our feelings regarding the problems that had arisen and to share the grief and disappointment resulting from the "unsatisfactory outcomes," to improve communication, and the need to establish a "Pediatric Cardiac Program Team." Great! This was all well and good. So we were all to sit in a room around a big table and talk about our feelings. Almost immediately, I felt the need to keep my mouth shut and my ears open, a strategy I had honed over the years while working in stressful situations. I listened to the other members of the Wiseman Committee. Most of the time I wondered why we were all there. No one had informed me as to why I was the only nurse there, or what I was supposed to do or say. So I sat. I listened. And I waited.

One of the things assigned to us was to make a list of our concerns. These were to be discussed at subsequent meetings. So the OR nurses got together one evening to discuss our concerns. We prepared a list and wrote them down. There were three areas of concern.

The first was communication. We mentioned our attempts to meet with Dr. Odim and get input on his specific needs. After the first two or three cases and hearing his complaints about cannulas, sutures and such, I had provided him with catalogues and encouraged him to let me know what he would like me to order. There was money allocated to the program, but if we didn't spend it, it could go elsewhere. I never heard back from him. At one point later on, Karin Dixon needed the catalogues back and called his office to have them returned. She called Dr. Odim, mentioning that the catalogues were being picked up, and asked if he had found anything that he wanted. He told her he hadn't had time to look at them.

The second concern was morale. We were greatly disturbed by the deaths of so many children in such a short period. The third concern was role confusion. I had directed Dr. Odim many times, showing him how to set things up, letting the perfusionists know when something was happening instead of waiting for him to announce it as was the usual routine—things that certainly were not in my job description. Initially, I had attributed this lack of knowledge to him being the "new guy." I wanted the perfusionists, who were male, to help out with this problem because I sensed that their assistance and comments would be better received. At one point, I asked Mike Maas, the head perfusionist, to stand at the top of the table during the cannulation process to make sure things were being done correctly. I didn't want that responsibility. I knew what should be done, but preventing the surgeon from making a mistake wasn't something I should have to do... at least, not on a regular basis.

Anesthesia presented their concerns at that meeting, and of course, communication was one. Another worry was that monitoring lines were changed in certain cases, and another was that the post-op chest X-ray did not happen. Dr. Duncan had always wanted it done before the patient left the OR. That way if there was a problem it could be addressed while the patient was still in the OR. Dr. Odim wanted the X-ray taken in the PICU in case a problem occurred during the transfer of the patient. Both reasons seemed valid, and I don't remember that issue ever being resolved.

Like the nurses, the anesthesiologists did not address surgical competence. I don't think any of us wanted to find out how that would be received. We needed to discuss it, but as the only nurse on the committee, I would never have brought it up. I hoped someone else would say something and then I planned to back them up. No one did. *Was I a coward?* I wrestled with that thought a few times. However, I knew I would be shot down immediately. There would be no real discussion.

The PICU attending's concerns were about the "surgical procedures" being done in the PICU and the lack of preparation, direction, and equipment for these events. He was referring to the closing Gary Caribou's chest and to the attempts to discontinue Jessica Ulimaumi's ECMO treatment in the PICU without any assistance from the OR. Dr. Odim had been asked several times for assistance regarding these issues but hadn't provided any; for example, the nurses set up and stocked a cardiac bin with no guidance from the surgeon.

Also, the rule in PICU was that once the patient was admitted there, the intensive care unit's attending doctor was in charge. Therefore, all orders and changes had to go through the attending. Dr. Odim had been advised of this policy, but he continued to try to bypass it. This caused confusion and tension with the nurses, who were to follow the orders left by the PICU doctor, not the surgeon. If these doctors disagreed on the care of the patient, they needed to sort it out amongst themselves.

Lastly, Dr. Odim seemed to expect a call from a night nurse with a report on his patients around 6 a.m. This is a common practice, but it is almost always a surgical resident that makes the call. This is a very busy time for the nurses as they are winding down from their night shift and getting ready to give report to the day staff. Also, they are getting the patients ready for the day, preparing them for scheduled tests or family comings and goings. The nurses didn't have the time at 6 a.m.

So these were some of the things discussed at the first meeting. It all felt awkward, and I sensed an underlying anger and disdain coming from Dr. Odim and Dr. Giddins. It was if they were trying to be patient with a bunch of people who just weren't as smart as them. Particularly Dr. Odim, who I felt, thought of himself as the smartest person in the room. It was as though they were humouring us, biding their time, going along with all this nonsense. As well, I felt that they blamed nursing and anesthesia for having to sit through these meetings. I was somewhat protected by Dr. Wiseman, just by the fact that we went back years. But I wasn't one hundred percent sure he would stick up for me if things got ugly. I would have to wait and see.

The anesthetists agreed to do low- and medium-risk cases and send the complex ones out. Since some patients were going to Saskatoon, it was decided that some members of the team should travel there to see how that team functioned. Dr. Odim seemed to think this was a good idea and so he, Dr. Jo Swartz, and I flew to Saskatoon for a couple of days. It was kind of amusing. Dr. Odim sat up in first class and Jo and I sat near the back of the plane in the "cattle car" as she put it. We did laugh about it. It seemed so typical.

Dr. Roxanne McKay was the surgeon there. She was a quick, efficient, and no-nonsense kind of surgeon. Her team seemed to be closely knit and they worked well together. Dr. Odim scrubbed in and assisted on two of the three cases she did while we were there. There were a few differences in the way the doctors approached the procedures, different instruments, sutures cannulas etc. Apart from a needle driver, an instrument that a surgeon uses to suture with, Dr. Odim did not express any interest in any of their instrumentation and equipment. I made a note to order the needle driver he liked and did so as soon as I returned to Winnipeg.

We returned to Winnipeg after two days; the key benefit of the trip was seeing another team work well together, but it only made me wish we had a surgeon like Dr. McKay. I don't know what her numbers were, but I doubt our kids would have been sent there if they weren't pretty good.

WITH ONE MEETING UNDER OUR BELTS and nothing resolved at that point, we carried on. The plan was to do low- and medium-risk cases and send the complex ones out … at least for the time being. Anesthesia had reluctantly agreed to this. Later, however, there would be discussions as to what constituted a low- to medium-risk case versus a high-risk procedure.

From my understanding, one of the criteria for "low" or "medium" risk is measured by the level of difficulty of the operation. This seemed to be the surgeon's and cardiologist's view. On the other hand, risk could also be measured by the condition of the child at the time of surgery: the risk posed to that particular child at that particular time. This seemed to be the position the anesthetists took. Their job was to assess the patient pre-operatively and care for the patient during the procedure. It could be argued that this was the more holistic view. Obviously, some of these children were very ill. Others were in relatively good shape. Sometimes the surgery had to be done at a precarious time, perhaps due to a sudden deterioration in the child's condition. So a relatively low-risk procedure could turn into something more difficult, requiring a higher level of skill. This was the basis of some of the discussions and disagreements between surgery and anesthesia. Aric Baumann, an eight-month-old baby with several cardiac problems, was a good example of how that difference of opinion between the anesthetists and the surgeon and cardiologist played out with tragic results. One of his problems was a condition called pulmonary hypertension, which meant the pressure of his pulmonary vessels (in his lungs) was too high. No one could figure out why. This raised his level of risk.

Throughout the month of June, the committee met on a weekly basis. There were no minutes taken.

AT THE JUNE 29 WISEMAN COMMITTEE MEETING, Jessica Ulimaumi was discussed. Dr. Reimer, the anesthetist, attended that meeting instead of Dr. McNeill because he was the anesthetist assigned to her operation. However, he was not in the PICU when she died. I knew that Jessica was going to be discussed at the meeting so I called Mike Maas to tell him to make sure one of the perfusionists would be there. Dave Smith, the perfusionist who had been at Jessica's bedside in the PICU that day, attended. The long pump and cross-clamp times and the leaking patch repair that had to be redone were discussed, along with some other issues.

When they got to the topic of weaning Jessica off the ECMO machine in the PICU, Dr. Odim made no mention of not clamping the cannula before it was removed, nor the fact that Jessica bled to death through that cannula and the cannula site. I was astounded. He said something to the effect that Jessica had bled to death, but without mentioning the actual reason. I was just about to ask him what had happened when, right at that point, Dave spoke up. This was a brave thing for him to do. He asked Dr. Odim directly for an explanation as to what had happened, stating that he was behind his machine and could not see what was happening at the site. Dr. Odim then explained that the cannula had not been clamped and that the child had exsanguinated (bled out) through it. He mentioned that Dr. Hancock was there and he had expected her to clamp the line because that would have been her job in the OR.

A discussion followed about the pros and cons of doing this kind of procedure in the PICU without any OR staff. Dr. Odim stated that he did not call the OR nurses in because he thought we didn't like to work on weekends. In fact, there were two OR nurses about one hundred steps away on the same floor. I'm pretty sure he knew that. I stated that it was certainly not true. I thought, but did not say, that Dr. Odim's reason was nonsense. Laughable. First of all, we always come in because there is always a nurse on call. We are paid to be on call on the weekends. It's part of our job. Most OR nurses are available. And surgeons know that. A couple I worked with seemed to take great pleasure in waking me at 3 a.m. One surgeon would always start the call by asking me what I was doing. Uh, sleeping?

We would have definitely come in for this. That day, the two nurses on duty had some cardiac experience and would have been capable of assisting. I don't think Dr. Odim wanted to bother calling them. Perhaps it was too much trouble to organize OR personnel, or perhaps he had something else to do that Sunday afternoon and didn't want to wait for the OR nurses. We will never know his reasons.

And so Jessica died. Surrounded by medical personnel with no family near her. Again, I felt so sad. She was a very fragile and sick little baby, and perhaps she wouldn't have survived even with the best of care. The point is, she didn't receive it.

At the meetings, it became clear that the tensions and animosity were only getting worse, definitely not better, as we were led to believe they would after everyone had aired their concerns. Dr. McNeill and I both felt this was evident. We had talked about it. In fact, as the summer went on, there was more tension building and there was definitely a push by Dr. Odim and Dr. Giddins to return to a full program. At one point, Dr. Odim seemed to think it was the anesthetists against everyone else on the committee. This certainly was not true.

CHAPTER 10

ARIC BAUMANN

Aric Baumann was operated on June 30, when he was eight months, fourteen days old. After spending fifty-two days in PICU following his surgery, he died on August 21.

He was born at St. Boniface Hospital on December 7, 1993. He was premature, born at thirty-two weeks gestation and weighing just five pounds, two ounces. Shortly after his birth, he was observed to be cyanotic (blue) and diagnosed with a heart murmur. He was seen there by Dr. Giddins and diagnosed with several other cardiac problems, including a partial AV (atrioventricular) canal. This meant he had a large hole in the middle of his heart which affected the mitral valve, the one between the left atrium and left ventricle, and the tricuspid valve, which sits between the right atrium and the right ventricle.

In a healthy heart, the left side of the heart is the main pumping chamber and has higher pressures, sending blood to the entire body. In Aric's case, the heart was pushing blood through the defect to the right side of the heart, which has lower pressures and normally sends blood to the lungs for oxygen. So now too much blood was going to the lungs and the child had what is known as pulmonary edema, meaning the lungs fill up with fluid and there's no room for the oxygen to get in. This is a somewhat oversimplified description of what happens, but it is a serious heart problem.

Initially, doctors thought that Aric could wait until he was two or three years of age before he needed surgery. However, he was noted to have difficulty breathing: his respirations were very fast and he had indrawing, a symptom of respiratory distress. Because a child's sternum is still soft, it can be seen to drawn in with each breath a sick child like Aric takes. He was treated for these symptoms with medications. Despite all this, he was gaining weight and seemed to be holding his own.

Aric and his parents attended Dr. Giddins's clinic several times in the subsequent months. On April 13, Aric came in for a follow-up visit with Dr. Giddins. He had deteriorated by then and he was scheduled for a heart catheterization in May. Dr. Giddins felt he might need surgery sooner rather than later. The heart catheterization showed several problems: the partial AV canal that had been diagnosed previously; a torrential left to right shunt, which meant that blood was pouring into the right side of his heart; severe right valve regurgitation, meaning that the defective valve could not handle the flow of blood coming in; and pulmonary hypertension, meaning the pressures in the vessels in his lungs were too high. The problem with the pulmonary hypertension was unusual and seemed to be getting worse and no one could figure out why it was happening.

Aric's parents met with Dr. Odim on June 16 to discuss their son's surgery. Both Dr. Giddins and Dr. Odim believed this operation to be low risk. However, with the pulmonary hypertension and torrential left to right shunting, Aric's operation would ultimately be deemed a much higher risk.

Later, it became clear that the Baumanns were never given complete information about the risk of the procedure or about the issues in the cardiac surgery program. Dr. Odim claimed that because most families asked about surgical dates, he told them that the program had slowed down and that there were problems within the team that they were trying to sort out. The Baumanns said that the slowdown was never mentioned and that Dr. Odim told them that the repair would take about fifteen minutes but the preparations in the OR beforehand could take several hours. They said that they did not receive any information about surgical risk.

Aric's surgery took five hours. At the end of the surgery, Aric's heart rhythm was irregular, demonstrating a conduction problem within the heart itself so pacemaker wires were hooked up. Pacemakers are an integral part in the recovery phase. Sometimes they are never needed and used, but they are always there to be a backup in case of problems. Putting in a temporary pacemaker can be fussy because the wires have to be placed on a precise spot on the surface of the heart. Aric's pacemaker failed to capture, which means the electrical impulses from the pacemaker were not hitting the correct spot within the heart to cause it to beat. This had become an ongoing problem in the ICUs with Dr. Odim's patients. Aric was put back on bypass. The wires were repositioned, again failing to capture, but after a few moments, Aric's heart started beating in a normal manner on its own.

Aric had an exceptionally long stay in the PICU. Fifty-two days on a ventilator. Pulmonary hypertension was the main issue, and no one seemed to be able to figure out why. Once the repair was done, it should have gone away. Finally, another cardiologist suggested an unusual problem that he had seen in his practice: pulmonary vein stenosis, a narrowing of the pulmonary vein, of which there are four, that brings oxygenated blood from the lungs to the left side of the heart.

Another cardiac catheterization was ordered and sure enough, a congenital pulmonary vein stenosis was identified. When compared with the first catheterization, done pre-operatively, it was noticeably more severe. It was not treatable. The only real option was a lung transplant, a procedure still in the early stages of development in the 1990s. Aric had no chance of surviving.

The doctors involved with Aric's care met with his family and discussed the fact that there were no treatment options left for Aric. There was nothing more they could do. Treatment was stopped and as the monitors started to show that things were slowing down, Aric's mother asked, "Is this it?" She was told it was. Aric died in his grandmother's arms at 11:34 a.m., August 21.

IN JULY, DR. ODIM PERFORMED an ASD repair on a seven-year-old. The repair was completed, and things were going pretty well until it was time to come off bypass. The anesthetist, Dr. Wong, alerted Dr. Odim to the fact that the child's blood oxygen levels were dropping. Each patient has a gadget called an Oximeter placed on their body, usually clipped or taped onto a finger. It measures the percentage of oxygen in the blood and ideally should be at one hundred percent or at least in the high nineties. Dr. Odim said that Dr. Wong must be having trouble ventilating the patient. Dr. Wong replied that the child was on one hundred percent oxygen and easy to ventilate with good air entry to her lungs. The breathing tube was properly positioned and oxygen was getting to the patient. So why was this happening?

Dr. Odim had another look and realized that there was a right to left shunt within the heart, which meant the ASD was still open. If the ASD (a hole between the left and right atria) is still open there will be blood flowing from right to left, which is not good. Blood to the body would have lower than normal oxygen levels. The child had to go back on bypass, the heart was re-opened, and it was discovered that Dr. Odim had sewn the eustachian valve (part of the heart's normal anatomy) shut instead of closing the ASD. This meant that low oxygenated blood was mixing with oxygenated blood and causing the problem with the oxygen levels. This was a big problem and meant that he had not done the repair correctly. The left side of the heart pumps blood out to the body, and it must be carrying oxygen to sustain life. The problem was corrected, the actual ASD was sutured closed, and the child did fine post-operatively.

However, Dr. Wong found this event to be extremely disturbing. I was not present for this operation but certainly heard about it afterward. It was discussed at the next Wiseman Committee meeting when Dr. McNeill brought it up. Both Drs. Giddins and Odim assured her that this was a recognized complication of this type of surgery, given the anatomy. Dr. Odim tried to explain how it was easy to mistake the eustachian valve for an ASD. Dr. Giddins offered to show her numerous journal articles on the subject. Subsequently, Dr. Wong looked for this complication in one of the pre-eminent textbooks on pediatric cardiac surgery. She could not find any mention of it. None of us had ever seen this happen before. Again, was Dr. Odim's knowledge of cardiac anatomy adequate?

The July 27 Wiseman Committee meeting was a contentious one. No minutes were taken, as usual. At this meeting, Dr. Giddins proposed a full resumption of the program. I was not at this meeting and had asked Carol Dupuis to attend it in my place. We had discussed what nursing felt about the resumption of a full program; if the issue were to come up, she was to say nursing did not feel comfortable going forward with high-risk cases. Drs. Giddins and Odim asked her for our reasons. She replied that too many things were still going wrong. Cannulation problems were one example, particularly the case where we had to go on "sucker bypass" after a cannula fell out. She also mentioned the problem with the eustachian valve mistake. At this, Dr. Giddins became upset and raised his voice. He said he could show her in a textbook that this was an easy mistake to make. Both he and Dr. Odim then went on to say (in so many words) that she was just a nurse and didn't know what she was talking about. However, she stuck to her guns and said that because of some of these incidents, nursing did not feel comfortable with resuming the full program. Dr. McNeill remembered that conversation and stated in court that both Dr. Giddins and Dr. Odim were quite dismissive of nursing concerns. At the end of the meeting, Dr. Wiseman told Carol that she was not making things any easier. However, the decision was made to hold off going to a full program for a bit longer. But the pressure was building week by week.

CHAPTER 11

SHALYNN PILLER

Shalynn Piller died on August 3, 1994, following a repair two days earlier of a coarctation (a narrowing) of her aorta. Of the twelve children who died, this was the one case that I was not involved in. I don't remember why, but since her surgery was in August, I was likely on vacation.

She was born in Carmen, Manitoba, a town south of Winnipeg, on July 20. About ten days later, she was taken by her parents to her family doctor because of their concerns regarding problems with feeding and irregular breathing. A loud heart murmur was heard on examination, and she was referred to Dr. Giddins at the Variety Heart Centre. She was admitted to the Children's Hospital. Further tests revealed an enlarged heart and decreased femoral pulses, which is a sign of poor circulation to the lower part of the body. She was diagnosed with a significant narrowing (coarctation) of the aorta, two VSDs, one of which was quite large, an abnormal tricuspid valve, and other cardiac issues related to these malformations. She would require surgery.

The Patent Ductus Arteriosus (PDA), a part of fetal circulation that remained open for a few days after her birth, had provided another route for the blood to get to her lower body. But now it was closing, a normal occurrence at this point. During their time in their mother's womb an infant does not breathe, so it is not using its lungs. The PDA is a large shunt between the pulmonary artery and the aorta. This allows the flow of blood to bypass the lungs and flow down the aorta to the umbilical artery and the placenta. Oxygenated blood is derived from the placenta and returns to the body by the umbilical vein. Soon after the child is born and starts to breathe, hormonal changes cause the PDA to close and the blood pressure in the body rises.

So Shalynn was in trouble. The blood to her lower body now had to make its way through this narrowed portion of the aorta, the closing ductus caused the heart to work harder against the obstruction and resulted in poor circulation to her liver, kidneys, intestines, legs and feet. She was treated with a drug called Prostaglandin—a hormone that could help keep her PDA open for the time being, thereby improving the circulation to her lower body—to buy time to figure out surgical options and treatment. She was admitted to the NICU later that day and was noted to be pale and to have cool and mottled lower extremities.

Shalynn's parents were told by the cardiologists who spoke to them about the surgical option that Dr. Odim was highly qualified and had come from the United States. They were not told of the slowdown or of any problems with the program. When Dr. Odim spoke to them, he told them that Shalynn's chances of survival with the surgery were around ninety-two percent. He did not tell them that she would require further surgery. In a letter to her family doctor, he said he thought that the repair of the VSD could wait until Shalynn was older. Dr. Giddins stated that he believed this surgery to be low risk because it was a closed heart operation, and the baby would not have to go on bypass.

Pre-operatively, she was stable, but her extremities were still mottled and cool and she was very irritable when handled. Her surgery was uneventful, and she was returned to the NICU in stable condition. The actual operation took about two-and-a half hours. Later that day, Shalynn suddenly deteriorated—her heart rate slowed, and she became unresponsive. She was given a drug called Atropine, which should have increased her heart rate. However, she did not respond to the drug. Her parents were called and told to come back to the hospital. Dr. Odim attended as well, and shortly after these first troubling signs, Shalynn had a cardiac arrest. A resuscitation was begun and lasted for several hours.

Early the following morning, concerns were raised about neurological damage. Tests were done, and the diagnosis of brain damage caused by lack of oxygen was confirmed. After a meeting on August 2 with staff and parents, a decision was made not to resuscitate Shalynn if she arrested again. Later the next day, treatment was withdrawn, and she died in her mother's arms at 6:25 p.m. August 3.

An autopsy was performed but no definitive cause of death was identified. The pathologist found that the repair was intact. There was some tissue death of the heart muscle noted, which could be explained by her cardiac arrest after surgery and the resuscitation. Why did she die? All this took place during the slowdown that summer.

ON AUGUST 10 THE COMMITTEE MET, and four matters were discussed. The first was case of a young child with tricuspid atresia who had to be returned to the OR with significant bleeding to have a central shunt put in. This child survived. The second was another discussion about the location of post-op care. The third was whether or not to go ahead with a specific patient who was deemed to be outside the parameters at the time and was deferred. The fourth was Dr. Wiseman's proposed Interim Report, which was presented to the Committee at the end of the meeting. It said:

> As a result of the frank and open discussion which occurred,
> a large number of problem areas were discovered, and spe-
> cific recommendations were made to improve the overall
> function of the team. Areas where problems appeared to
> arise included many items relating to team communication.
> A significant amount of discussion was devoted to improved
> communication between nursing, surgery, anesthesiology,
> and bypass technology. It was felt that this frank discussion
> resulted in paving the way for much improved communi-
> cation in the future.

Dr. Wiseman also discussed specific areas where changes could be made. They included:

The effective use of invasive monitoring lines so as to satisfy the requirement of both anesthesiology and to meet the needs of post-operative monitoring.

Specific technical details concerning team communication relating to going on cardiopulmonary bypass and coming off cardiopulmonary bypass.

Methodology and communication concerning the administration of anti-coagulation agents and agents for reversals of anti-coagulation.

Details relating to transfer of patients from operating room to Intensive Care Unit and with respect to this the timing of a post-operative radiogram.

Details concerning the use of cardioplegia solutions.

Specific recommendations concerning the timing and ordering of blood products for use at the conclusion of cardiopulmonary bypass. Products to be ordered from the Red Cross for availability immediately coming off of bypass.

The recognition that the operating room assistant is a major component to the smooth and safe conduct of the surgical procedure. A group of such assistants familiar with the Children's Hospital personnel and operating theater is gradually developed.

The need for an operating room call-back system in the event of re-operation taking place in the Intensive Care Unit. As well the need for instrumentation for re-operation under emergency circumstances in the Intensive Care Unit.

The need to recognize that specific cases of greater complexity not be undertaken using the early experience of the

Program. It was the consensus of the committee that the
early experience included cases that exceeded the program
maturity at its onset.

The report also stated that the team was able to "work together and
during this period of time, significant success was met."

The improvement in team dynamics happened, in my opinion, because
we were doing low- and medium-risk cases only. There was no mention
of the mortality and morbidity rates or what led to them.

The report contained no recommendations. It concluded by saying:

After considerable Team discussion and with some degree of
trepidation it was recommended that the overall approach
to the Cardiac Program occur with the development of a
staging system based upon complexity and risk involved
with individual cases.

In the final copy of the report the word "Trepidation" was replaced
with the word Reservations.

Nowhere was there any mention of the concerns that nursing and
anesthesia had about the competency of the surgeon. Of course, they
had never been discussed at any meeting that I had been present at. I
felt uneasy, especially after the way Carol Dupuis had been treated when
she raised nursing concerns at the July 27 meeting. Dr. McNeill felt the
same way. We were viewed as being obstructive by Drs. Giddins, Odim,
and Wiseman. None of us had the credentials that Dr. Odim had and
when he dismissed our concerns, that was the end of the discussion. As
the summer wore on, we all concluded that the return to high-risk cases
was inevitable. The pressure to resume was intensifying.

Daniel Terziski's case was discussed at the next meeting on August 24.
There was a discussion about the post-op care in the NICU. The committee concluded that all open-heart cases should go to the PICU for
their post-op care.

Further discussions at that meeting concluded that the program should
return to full service (take all comers) in two weeks, even though it had

not been proposed in the Interim Report. This decision was definitely rushed. On July 27, the consensus was to continue with low-risk cases only. On August 10, it had been recommended that full-service resume in four to six months. Despite the two deaths (Shalynn and Aric) and review of the Terziski case, Dr. Wiseman informed the committee on August 24 that he was recommending full-service return in two weeks time.

At a meeting of the department of anesthesia, Drs. Wong, Reimer, Swartz, and McNeill reluctantly agreed to go back to full service. My understanding of their decision was that they felt any further resistance was futile.

On September 7, the Wiseman Committee met again. Several discussions took place, including information about children who had been sent out over the summer slowdown. Fourteen patients had surgery elsewhere. Three of those patients had died. Dr. Wiseman believed that the HSC program was "weakened" by the reduction of the number of complex cases.

So the full-service program resumed.

CHAPTER 12

MARIETESS TENA CAPILI

"My rights as a parent to do the best for my child were taken away from me."

So said Marietess's father, Ben Capili. He and Sarah Tena were the young parents of two-year-old Marietess.

Marietess had a very serious and complex heart malformation. Her heart and the vessels going to and coming from it were not normal. At about six months of age, she had had an operation to put in a shunt that would redirect some of the blood flow to her lungs. This was performed by Dr. Duncan and had gone well. However, she would need another operation to fix several problems with her cardiac anatomy. The plan was to do it when Marietess was about three years of age. She was becoming more cyanotic (blue), she tired easily when playing, and had other signs of heart failure. She needed surgery. Marietess's grandmother broached the idea of the surgery being done in Toronto. The child of an acquaintance had undergone surgery there successfully. She was assured by both Dr. Giddins and Dr. Odim that it could be done safely in Winnipeg. Because the surgery Dr. Duncan performed had gone well, they agreed.

These conversations took place in August 1994, during the time we were doing low- to medium-risk cases only. However, around that time, the decision had been made to "take all comers" again.

Parents of a critically ill child who is going for surgery are going through an extremely stressful time. They want to make the best decisions for their child often in a short period of time. It is a huge responsibility for anyone to make lifesaving decisions for someone you love more than you love yourself. But how can someone with no "in" to the medical system find someone who might know something, perhaps a nurse or doctor outside the program who might have heard about what was going on. Is the onus on the people who are part of this program, which had been shut down, to alert the parents to this fact?

Ben said later that if he had known about the shutdown during that summer, he never would have consented to the surgery taking place in Winnipeg. "If they had told me that it had closed down we would have gone (to Toronto) right off the bat. Once you heard that a program has shut down, you wouldn't want anything to do with it." There was never any mention of the shutdown and the reasons for it to Ben and Sarah before the operation. And that is a big part of the tragedy.

And so, on September 13, Marietess went to the OR. She was in the OR for eleven hours and fifty-six minutes. I was there with her the whole time.

The operative report is a description of the surgery performed and is usually dictated by the surgeon immediately after the surgery, sometimes into a phone right in the OR. Dr. Odim's report stated that Marietess underwent an anastomosis (joining) of the superior vena cava to the pulmonary artery; the enlargement of the septal opening between the two atria; the take down of the BT shunt that Dr. Duncan had created earlier in her life; and the closure of the Patent Ductus Arteriosus (PDA), a part of the fetal circulation that usually closes off at birth but was kept open because of the problems with Marietess's malformed heart.

There were numerous problems. One of the first things that happened was a problem with cannulation. As I watched Dr. Odim try to insert the cannula into the vena cava, I mentioned quietly that I thought the cannula was too big. He didn't seem to hear my comment and tore the vessel. He backed off, sutured it and put in another purse string suture, and retried with another smaller cannula. This caused a lot of bleeding and necessitated blood transfusions. Later, Dr. Odim seemed to blame the anesthetist. He stated that she should have been prepared for this event by administering a "volume overload" in case there was bleeding, thereby reducing the chance of a drop in pressures due to potential blood loss while he was cannulating. How did this make sense? Did he mean he knew he was likely going to tear a vessel and we should all be prepared? Another cannula was inserted, and the pump started. Immediately the perfusionist announced that the blood flow was low. As the circulating nurse that day, I was watching everything carefully. It was then that the anesthetist and I observed that one of the two venous cannulas that take the blood from the patient to the bypass machine was still clamped. I let the team know immediately, the clamp was removed, and the blood flow increased.

Later, the anesthetist noted that Marietess's heart was swelling up with blood. There had been a drain placed in the heart to prevent this from happening and apparently Dr. Odim had removed or dislodged it. It was replaced and that problem was solved. There was a lot of bleeding. She was bleeding from the anastomosis Dr. Odim had created and also from a coagulopathy (failure of clotting) probably due to medications given to prevent the blood from clotting while on bypass. These problems were addressed by the surgeon and the anesthetist.

The big problem was that Marietess's head and face became swollen and purple toward the end of the procedure. The superior vena cava (SVC) had been cannulated and sutured to the pulmonary artery to divert blood flow from the upper body to the lungs. Now there was a problem known as SVC Syndrome. This means that the heart pumps blood to the upper part of the body, but the return route, the superior vena cava that returns oxygen-depleted blood to the heart, is obstructed for some reason. So the blood was going to Marietess's head but had no way to get back. This beautiful child was unrecognizable. As the surgical drapes were pulled back, I was shocked and horrified by her appearance.

A discussion ensued because of a difference of opinion between the anesthetist and the surgeon. Dr. Swartz believed that the cause was something mechanical, an obstruction of the SVC, which had been cannulated and sutured and manipulated during the surgery. Dr. Odim seemed to think that it was drug-related, that adrenalin given by Dr. Swartz had caused vasoconstriction, a spasm or narrowing of the vessel. He did not want to keep the child in the OR any longer.

Before leaving with Marietess, Dr. Swartz suggested doing a test to see if the vessel was blocked. This entailed injecting a radio-opaque dye into the vessel and taking an X-ray. Dr. Giddins was consulted, and he agreed with Dr. Odim. So against Dr. Swartz's strong recommendation to keep her in the OR until the cause of the problem was identified, Marietess was transferred to the PICU.

Again, here was an example of Dr. Odim letting a patient leave the OR before ascertaining what the problem was and dealing with it. It was also against the advice of the anesthetist, who should have had a say. It was so obvious something was terribly wrong. SVC Syndrome is a serious condition and there is always a reason for it. Find it. Deal with it. I was so scared for this child when I saw her, and I know other members of the team were as well.

When her parents first saw her after her surgery on September 13, she was unrecognizable, her face was so swollen and discoloured. They were shocked and distressed at the sight of their beautiful little girl. They spoke to Dr. Odim and Dr. Giddins and were told that her condition was serious but were not told that she might not survive the night. After visiting Marietess briefly, Ben headed home for a few hours sleep. Sarah and her mother stayed at the hospital. Over the next few hours, Marietess's condition continued to deteriorate. Around 2 a.m., Sarah called Ben and told him to come back to the hospital. They sat in the PICU waiting room. A short time later Dr. Giddins and Dr. Odim came in and told them that Marietess had died.

At autopsy, an obstruction of the SVC was located at the site where the difficult cannulation and purse string resuturing had occurred. Later at the inquest, witnesses were generally in agreement that it had been a mistake to move Marietess to the PICU without determining the cause of the SVC Syndrome. One expert witness went so far as to say, "I would have locked the door."

Surgeons are required to write a letter and a report to the referring doctor after any operation. In his letter to Dr. Grewer, Marietess's physician, Dr. Odim described her condition as "satisfactory but critical" and he neglected to mention several important issues that arose during the surgery. Everyone involved in the case felt that there was nothing satisfactory about Marietess's condition when she arrived in the PICU.

This was so tragic and so preventable. So many "shoulda, coulda, wouldas" were swirling around in my head. At the time of the surgery, I had no idea what the parents had been told or not told. I was still trying to come to terms with the idea that we were going back to a full program and taking all the cases coming through the door.

A couple of years later, I was asked to speak at an event for nurses. Two or three of the nurses involved in this had been asked to come and talk about what was then a well-known national news story. Ben Capili was there and approached me. I recognized him, but he introduced himself anyway. He had come to hear us, and we spoke briefly. I wasn't sure what he was going to say to me, and I was a little apprehensive. However, he was sweet and kind, saying that he did not blame me or the other nurses for what had happened. He had come to understand that we had tried to bring attention to the problems but that no one had been willing to listen at the time. I have no idea what I said to him other than *thank you*.

There were many times when I felt that somehow, I was partly to blame for this whole thing. Especially after the media got hold of the story. One parent said that the nurses should have said or done something earlier. Later, after hearing more about what we tried to do, she said she understood. I know now that I wasn't to blame, but when one is so deeply involved, many different thoughts and emotions swirl around in your brain. As medical caregivers, we take that responsibility seriously. When things don't go well, of course we feel varying degrees of blame.

I certainly vacillated between guilt, remorse, feeling responsible, and feeling like a victim myself. Everything was so mixed up. I know the other nurses were going through the same thing. We had each other and by then a team of psych nurses who deal with employees undergoing stress and grief were there to debrief us.

In November 1994, Ben Capili finally arranged a meeting with Dr. Giddins. Ben attended with his mother-in-law Teresida Tena. Marietess's mother declined to come. Dr. Odim was not present. The autopsy report was not yet completed at that time and the family did not receive it until February 1995. They were told by Dr. Giddins that Marietess died as a result of fluid in her lungs.

When Ben asked about Dr. Odim's level of skill and ability, Dr. Giddins told them that Dr. Odim had trained in Boston and Montreal. I was surprised to hear this. By now, I would have thought that Dr. Giddins would have had his own questions and concerns about Dr. Odim's surgical skill. I hoped that he had made it past the dazzling credentials, the fancy schools, the twenty-five-page CV to the realities of Dr. Odim's skills or lack thereof. I never understood this. However, I remember someone telling me that although Dr. Giddins was a well-trained cardiologist, he didn't really have a clue as to what actually happened in the OR. This opinion came from someone who knew him well. To me it seemed that people wanted this program to succeed no matter what the cost. A cardiac program is a very prestigious thing for a large medical centre. As a member of the program, I wanted it to succeed too. After Marietess, I was certain that darker days were ahead but even so, I wasn't prepared for what was to come.

On September 23, the Wiseman Committee met again. Much of the meeting was spent discussing the One Team-One Location idea whereby all post-op care would take place in the PICU with the NICU staff participating. I had made some notes about Marietess's case and had given them to Dr. Wiseman prior to the meeting. At the end of the meeting, he pushed them toward me, indicating I could speak about the case if I wanted to. I had expected him to start the discussion and was shocked when it seemed to fall on me to do so. I had seen so many unpleasant things happen at the meetings by then that I opted to remain silent. There was no way I was going to speak out. To me it seemed futile to do so. By then nurses had been silenced.

By the end of September, nursing was distressed. The PICU nurses had not been informed of the decision to take on all cases. When they realized that this was happening, there was an increase in anxiety within the unit. They expected these high-risk kids to come to their unit in poor condition. So many complications, open chests, and pacing problems made some nurses feel sick and struggle just to come to work. Seeing the parents suffering too caused a great deal of heartache for the staff. It was the stuff of nightmares.

CHAPTER 13

ERICA BICHEL

Erica was born on September 29, 1994, at thirty-six weeks gestation. At first she seemed fine. She was pink, active, and alert. Once she started to breathe, her PDA started to close as it should. But over the next twenty-four hours, Erica began to display symptoms of cardiac failure. Her colour became dusky, she had trouble feeding, and her respiration rate increased. She was in trouble. At about forty hours of age, she was transferred to the NICU where she was diagnosed with several life-threatening congenital defects.

They included tricuspid atresia (an underdeveloped valve on the right side of her heart), an ASD (a hole between the right and left atria), an abnormal pulmonary vein, a transposition of the great arteries (the aorta and the pulmonary artery were coming off the wrong ventricles), a under-developed aortic arch with a coarctation (a narrowing of the aorta), a small VSD (a hole between the right and left ventricles), and a severely hypoplastic (underdeveloped) right side of her heart. On its own, each one of these defects was going to cause Erica trouble; together they posed a serious threat to her life. In order for her to survive, she would need surgery within a few days.

Dr. Ward, the cardiologist who examined Erica, described her as "catastrophically unwell." Drug therapy was started to increase the pumping ability of her heart. She needed a Modified Norwood operation, a high-risk and complex cardiac procedure. We had done one on Daniel Terziski and it had resulted in a "poor outcome," a term Drs. Odim and Giddins liked to use. Daniel had died.

Dr. Odim examined Erica shortly after and deemed her very high-risk because of the resuscitative efforts including the drug therapy she had required. He spoke to her parents to explain the procedure and he described the risk as about fifty/fifty. Erica's father asked him if he had ever performed this procedure and Dr. Odim stated that he had assisted on several during his training. He did not inform them of the Daniel Terziski case, or of any alternatives to surgery in Winnipeg, such as transferring Erica out to another centre. The parents agreed to the procedure. I am sure I would have made the same decision if faced with the same information.

It was all so tragic.

There are times when I think about what these parents went through and the decisions they had to make. I struggled to decide whether or not to send my child to French Immersion, which by comparison seems to be a mundane decision. In Canada, we have two official languages, French and English, and we can educate our children in either one. The children go to different schools. Next door, my son's friend, who was the same age as my son, went to a different school because he was in the English program. The difference is that I had time to make that decision and the resources to research it thoroughly. My child's life was not in the balance. I cannot imagine the stress the parents went through and the incredible sadness and guilt they experienced, likely forever after, at the loss of the one they loved most in the world. The parents of some of these children had hours or days to make a life and death decision without all the information they would need.

Erica began to deteriorate even more. Her situation was becoming desperate. She was becoming more and more reliant on the medications to maintain her blood pressure and cardiac activity. She was taken to the

OR on October 4, 1994. She was in very bad shape. She was intubated and on a ventilator. The settings on the ventilator had to be adjusted constantly to deal with her increasing oxygen requirements. She was just so sick. The risks of surgery were astronomically high. Despite all this, the NICU staff were never given specific instructions or protocols from Dr. Odim regarding Erica's care and therefore were not sufficiently prepared to care for such a sick baby. My question would be, why not go in and ask the staff if there is anything more they need to know?

Dr. Odim performed a ligation of the PDA, an atrial septectomy (removal of the wall between the right and left atria), an insertion of a right BT shunt (a small shunt is placed between the innominate artery, an artery that branches off of the aortic arch, and the right pulmonary artery) and a homographic augmentation of the aorta (rebuilding the narrowed aorta using a tissue graft harvested from an organ donor). Erica was in the operating room for nine hours and forty minutes. The actual operation took seven hours and fifteen minutes. She was put on circulatory arrest for one hour and forty minutes and bypass time was three hours and thirty-two minutes. All these times are lengthy and pose serious problems post-operatively.

The total circulatory arrest (TCA) time was very long. This also raised issues with the protection of Erica's myocardium (heart muscle) as the blood supply to it had been suspended. In order to do this, the patient is cooled down to about 16 to 20 degrees C (normal body temperature is around 37 degrees C). The heart stops with cardioplegia, a procedure whereby a catheter is inserted into the aortic root and, without getting too technical, a cold solution is injected continuously through the coronary arteries during the time the heart is stopped. It is given every thirty minutes to keep the heart from beating. This is to perfuse and protect the heart muscle itself. Injury to the brain was also a concern.

In his notes, Dr. Odim stated that cardioplegia was administered. However, the perfusionist's record does not reflect this, and it is their responsibility to run it in at the surgeon's order. Todd Koga, one of the perfusionists, stated that he had no record or memory of giving the solution. The use of cardioplegia in this type of case is controversial because it is usually run in through a tiny cannula at the root of the aorta, which in Erica's case was extremely small and, because of all the medications she had received, thin and easily damaged. At the end of the operation, several attempts were made to wean Erica off bypass. Each time she deteriorated rapidly and had to be placed back on. After the third or fourth attempt and several resuscitative drugs, and in consultation with Drs. Odim, Giddins, Ward and a neonatologist, the team decided that nothing further could be done. Erica died in the OR at 4:30 p.m.

Erica's parents had been at home and in communication with Lois Hawkins, a nurse from the Variety Heart Centre. They were told to return to the hospital and shortly after they arrived, they were told that Erica had died.

Everything changes in the OR when a child dies. It becomes quiet. During the case several monitors are beeping, music might be playing, people are speaking and discussing treatment options and the activity level is high. Once the child has passed away, the music and the monitors are turned off. All the noise ceases. The conversations are minimal, and voices are quiet and soft. Usually, the physicians and perfusionists leave the room, leaving the nurses with the patient. Someone fills a basin with warm soapy water and the child is bathed, most of the tubes are removed or tied off and the baby is wrapped in a cozy blanket. Then, one of us carries the child back to the unit and places her into the loving arms of her family. Nurses describe this as the worst part of our job. Having done it a few times, I really can't think of anything worse.

The autopsy findings showed heart muscle and brain damage, which could have occurred before Erica even went to the OR. Questions arose as to whether Erica should have been operated on sooner, or at all. Many other aspects of the case were discussed at length and there were several opinions. One of the most important ones was whether the team had been ready and capable of embarking on a procedure of this magnitude.

Somewhere around this time, I made a conscious effort not to be the nurse who would go down to the waiting room and take the child from its parents' arms and take it into the OR. I just couldn't do it anymore. When we do that, we chat with the parents for a bit, trying to be upbeat and friendly because we know they are terrified, and as we leave with their child, we tell them they'll see each other soon. I felt awful, like I was lying to these people. Even though I was a stranger, they trusted me and handed their child over. It was a horrible feeling. Since I was the nurse in charge of the cardiac operating room, I was there for almost every case, including those of the surviving children. I was seeing all the problems on a regular basis, and it got to be too much.

SOMETIME IN SEPTEMBER, Dr. Andrew Hamilton was hired as an adult cardiac surgeon at the HSC. Because his training had included pediatric surgery, he was expected to spend about fifteen percent of his practice performing pediatric cardiac surgery, providing relief for Dr. Odim. We all found Dr. Hamilton to be a very competent and confident surgeon. Things went more smoothly, and he communicated well with the team. I always felt more comfortable when he was in the room. Although he was young, he seemed to be more experienced and confident than Dr. Odim. He had an air of authority and conducted himself professionally at all times. He was assertive and on a couple of occasions he corrected Dr. Odim. On one occasion he came in toward the end of a problematic case to help. Someone had called him. As he was gowning and gloving, he asked me what the problem was. I told him it was a bleeding problem. He told me to warm up the Tisseal. Tisseal is a surgical adhesive. It comes in powder form and is mixed with a solution and warmed up before it is applied to a bleeding site. It seals off the tissues. Hence the name. I reminded Dr. Hamilton that Dr. Odim did not like to use Tisseal. He simply said, "He'll use it this time." And he did.

At some point he was directed by Dr. Blanchard and Dr. Unruh to assist in all high-risk and neonatal cases in the future. This meant that he would have to be informed of the cases as they came in. Apparently this arrangement was never communicated to Dr. Odim.

THE WISEMAN COMMITTEE MET AGAIN ON OCTOBER 17. Most of the meeting discussions again revolved around the transferring of NICU patients to the PICU for post-op care. The neonatal nurses were quite resistant to this change, however. They had prepared post-operative care packages and guidelines of managing the care of these patients in the NICU. Again, there were negative feelings regarding Dr. Odim's lack of input regarding care plans for his post-op patients. Dr. Kesselman remarked that he believed there would have to be two nurses assigned to these cases, one from the PICU and one from the NICU.

Interestingly there was no discussion about the team attempting Norwood operations, although at some point Dr. Odim remarked that Dr. Wiseman did not approve of them being done under any circumstances. Erica's case was not discussed either.

The committee did not meet again until December 7, after yet another infant had died in the OR.

CHAPTER 14

ASHTON FEAKES

One weekend in the fall of 1994, my nine-year-old son Joshua and I were at a local shopping mall. As per usual, we stopped off at the food court for something unhealthy to eat. As we sat at our table eating our chicken fingers and fries, I noticed a family at the next table. They had a toddler in a highchair right beside us and as we sat there, I could see him eyeing Josh's fries and just then, he reached over as if he was trying pick one up. His parents noticed this too and grabbed his arm just in time. We smiled at each other.

This little guy had Down Syndrome. He was about a year and half old, blond, and very cute. I wondered if he had any problems with his heart. Since this was in the fall of 1994, I hoped not. Kids with Downs often have congenital heart defects. These children often need cardiac surgery at an early age. I had seen several of them come through our OR over the years. Most did well.

A couple of weeks later I was scrubbing my hands at the sinks outside the OR, getting ready for another one of Dr. Odim's cases when the circulating nurse walked by with Ashton Feakes in her arms.

Ashton Feakes was born in Winnipeg on July 15, 1993. Shortly after his birth, he was diagnosed with a heart murmur and congestive heart failure. He was treated for this and sent home. His mother Linde met with Dr. Giddins and was told that he would need surgery and that it would likely take place in Toronto or some other major centre. This was around the time Dr. Duncan had left Winnipeg and before Dr. Odim arrived. So that made sense. Investigations showed that Ashton had a right aortic arch, which meant that as his aorta rose out of the left ventricle it curved to the right, instead of curving to the left as in a normal heart; a complete AV (atrioventricular) canal, which meant that the valves between the upper and lower chambers of the heart, the atria and ventricles respectively, were malformed and disrupted; bilateral ventricular hypertrophy, meaning his ventricles were enlarged and mild valve regurgitation (a back wash of blood flow); and several other related problems. The bottom line was that blood flowing through the heart could not go by its normal routes.

These defects would require surgery to correct. Dr. Giddins decided to wait until Ashton was a little older before attempting surgery. Later that year, Ashton had a couple of bouts of pneumonia which were concerning and were treated with antibiotics.

In the spring of 1994, after speaking with Dr. Giddins, Ashton's parents were under the impression that he would be having surgery fairly soon. However, he still had several bouts of pneumonia and was in and out of Children's Hospital for treatment. So he was not in optimal condition for surgery. In April, his case was presented at the CVT conference for consideration for surgery.

Dr. Odim met with the parents in May 1994. By then, the anesthetist-mandated slowdown was on, but this fact was not mentioned to Ashton's parents. Because of this and because of the severity of his case, Ashton was not a candidate for surgery at this time. Dr. Odim explained the operative procedure and risks involved to Ashton's parents. However, Linde Feakes had the impression that the risks were low, (ninety-nine percent success rate) and that this was a "run-of-the-mill" type of surgery. During a meeting with Dr. Odim, Ashton's parents were told that their son's chances were about eighty percent if he were operated on in a world-class heart centre. In a further discussion with Dr. Odim, they were informed that he had come from one of those world-class centres (Boston), so they took that to mean he was a person capable of doing this type of operation. Initially, Ashton's father, John, had wanted the surgery done elsewhere, but he was now convinced that it could be done by Dr. Odim in Winnipeg.

Was Dr. Odim being deceptive? Hard to say. He certainly, according to Ashton's parents, seemed to give the impression that he was experienced and capable. Also, they had been under the impression that the surgery would be done over the summer. When they inquired about why it wouldn't be done then, they were told that there was a backlog of cases, not that there was a slowdown. Dr. Giddins later claimed that he had withheld this information because "it had no pertinence to Ashton's surgical care in the future." Because Ashton's dad had wanted him sent out for surgery, I would disagree with that statement: it certainly was a pertinent bit of information which could have changed the course of things, had Ashton's parents known. Even though other children had been sent out of town over the summer, Ashton was not.

In September 1994, Ashton was scheduled for surgery in October. However, Ashton had several health problems during the fall which required his operation to be postponed and he did not go to the OR until November 1, 1994, when he was sixteen months old. At that point, he was considered a higher risk patient.

His operation was long and involved. He was in the OR for eight hours and twenty-two minutes. The operation itself seemed to go very well without any technical concerns.

This was a big operation for a little guy like Ashton. On November 5, after doing fairly well for the first few days, he began to deteriorate. From that point on, he never really recovered. His post-op problems included a lung infection, mitral valve regurgitation, and heart rhythm problems. Ashton had heart block postoperatively and he was paced for that problem.

A day or so later, on November 4, Ashton had mild to moderate mitral regurgitation (backup of blood through the mitral valve). On

November 6 a chest X-ray showed pulmonary edema (fluid in the lungs) and his oxygen levels started to drop over the next twenty-four hours. On November 7, another chest X-ray showed collapse of the upper lobe of his right lung. He now had severe mitral valve regurgitation and his mitral valve no longer functioned. A mitral valve replacement (another big operation requiring bypass) was considered, but deemed too risky at that time. A wait-and-see plan was put in place. If Ashton could tolerate the problem with his mitral valve with medication, a replacement would not be necessary. All alternatives to surgery had to be considered first.

On November 9, Ashton took a turn for the worse. His oxygen saturations started to drop and it was difficult to keep his lungs clear of secretions. As well, his platelet count was dropping. The next day, Ashton suffered a hemorrhage from his lungs. He was now past the point of consideration for a valve replacement. His oxygen saturation dropped even further and pink frothy secretions were suctioned from his lungs. He was in pulmonary edema (a backup of blood in his lungs) from the severe mitral regurgitation. An echocardiogram showed a small leak in the VSD patch, mitral regurgitation, and significant shunting of blood from the left to right side of his heart. He was examined by several specialists. His kidneys shut down, and he was dialyzed once. He was started on several antibiotics. Nothing seemed to work.

Ashton's parents were told that he would likely not survive very long and at 8:27 p.m. on November 11, Ashton passed away with his family present at his bedside.

Ashton was the same little boy I had seen at the mall. When I saw him being carried into the OR, I recognized him. My knees felt weak, I felt slightly nauseated and to this day, I wish I had said something right then and there. *Stop! Take him back. Give him back to his parents. I will come and talk to them.* All those thoughts went through my head at once. What good would that have done?

CHAPTER 15

JESSE MAGUIRE

It was Saturday, November 20, 1994, the day before Grey Cup Sunday. I'm not much of a football fan. I never really understood the game. My husband would watch it, and I would walk in now and then to ask who was winning, but that would be the extent of my interest. No big party with beer, chips and dip, and other tasty snacks for us. We were going to spend that day at home.

Then the phone rang. It was work.

One of the two nurses working in the OR that weekend was calling. She informed me that Dr. Odim had scheduled an emergency case the next day. A newborn who would require a repair to his aorta and would need to be put on bypass was in the NICU. Could I come in? She was laughing as she spoke to me, and I asked her what was so funny. She told me that when Dr. Odim booked the case, she told him she would call me or one of the other cardiac nurses. He said he felt they could manage without us.

I was dumbstruck when I heard this. She was a fairly junior nurse, as was the other nurse on that day. Neither had much exposure to cardiac surgery and she found it odd that he wouldn't want his experienced team. She was kind of incredulous. As she spoke to me, it was like she couldn't really believe it.

To me this was another example of Dr. Odim's lack of understanding of nursing roles, and perhaps his lack of respect for the nurses he worked with. Taking it further, thinking about some of his comments to me and other female members of the team, I wondered about his disrespect for women in general. He just didn't get it and was not interested in understanding the roles of the nurses he worked with or their areas of expertise. I always felt that he thought of us as generic or interchangeable. I felt annoyed that Dr. Odim would put these nurses in such a dangerous position, just because he didn't like me. Both were very competent but had almost zero cardiac experience. At least they recognized their limitations and called me. I said I'd come in and asked them to call another cardiac nurse as well.

I just couldn't figure it out. Any surgeon wants the best and most highly capable people working beside him. Especially for a difficult or complex case. I knew Dr. Odim had not worked with the nurses on duty, at least in any major case—he didn't know them—so I had to wonder how he thought they would cope. Was he planning to train them as they went along? While this child was on bypass? Later the next day, as I was setting up the OR, Dr. Odim walked in. He spied me and asked me what I was doing there. I don't remember exactly what I said, but my reply was short and not particularly sweet. He did not seem happy to see me, but I didn't care. I felt the same way about him. Our relationship was now past the point of repair.

I have worked with surgeons that I dislike or who I thought disliked me. My way of dealing with this was to say as little as possible, keep a low profile, and do my job. The OR is no place for a fight. In any workplace we run into people that we don't particularly like. That's life. Medicine is no different. No big deal. Just get the work done and go home.

Jesse was two days old. He was born at the HSC and almost immediately the doctors noticed some respiratory distress, pale colour, and bluish fingers and toes. He was checked over and a pediatric cardiologist was consulted. He was diagnosed with a number of heart defects. They included an interrupted aortic arch; a malformation of the aortic valve;

a PFO (patent foramen ovale, part of the fetal circulation), an opening between the upper chambers of the heart that usually closes shortly after birth; a large VSD; an enlarged left atrium; and a PDA.

Clearly, Jesse required surgery as soon as possible. There were three options.

One was to do a "two-stage repair" which was to deal with the most urgent problem—the interrupted (underdeveloped) aortic arch—and leave the VSD for a later date. Another was to put a band around the pulmonary artery to slow the flow of blood to the lungs, fix the aortic arch, and leave the VSD for another time. Both of these procedures could be done without going on bypass. The third option was to do everything in one operation, which meant going on bypass. It would also mean putting the baby into total circulatory arrest (TCA) which meant cooling the baby's body temperature, stopping everything including the bypass machine in order to have a blood-free operative field, and then, as quickly as possible, complete the repair.

All three were very risky. The cardiologist was recommending the two-stage repair in order to allow the baby a chance to grow a bit before closing the VSD. However, there could be risks down the road from this.

Not surprisingly, Dr. Odim's decision was the third, and riskiest, option, do it all in one operation. I suppose a fourth option could have been to send the baby out. That, to my knowledge, was never discussed with Jesse's parents. Later in court, when asked if he considered this option, Dr. Odim stated that it never crossed his mind.

Dr. Odim discussed his decision to do the one-stage procedure with the cardiologist, Dr. Ward, who had some reservations. He felt that the first part of the two-stage procedure was fairly low-risk and why not wait for the child to grow a bit and get bigger and stronger before doing the second part. But Dr. Odim was adamant, saying that two, maybe three procedures would be necessary in the future and that this posed a higher risk to the child. That day there were two cardiologists involved in Jesse's care pre-operatively and both were used to seeing the more conservative two-stage method. Though Dr. Hamilton could perhaps have been of assistance in this high-risk surgery, he was never called in.

Dr. Odim had seen five or six of these one-stage procedures during his training. He did not tell the parents that he had never actually done this operation on his own. Jesse's mother, Laurie, later described Dr. Odim as he spoke to them about the operation. She characterized him as relaxed, leaning back in his chair with his hands clasped behind his head. He seemed very confident. No one told the parents about the problems within the program, nor were they offered the option of transferring Jesse to a larger centre for surgery.

So it began. We got the room ready for Jesse. When he came in, he was in an isolette (incubator), which was keeping him cozy and warm. He had several lines, IVs, and monitoring devices hooked up to him, so it was quite a complicated process to extricate him from the incubator. Finally, the circulating nurse was able to lift him out and place him on the bed. The room and the bed had been warmed up, but it wasn't as warm as the isolette and Jesse became agitated and started to cry. I was touched as I watched the circulating nurse tuck warm blankets around him and lean over him, nearly covering him with her body. She spoke softly to him, stroked his cheek, and he settled.

This was one of the darkest days of my career. I try not to think about it very often. It was literally my worst nightmare come true. It was what I had feared would happen one day. To this day, nearly thirty years later, I still think about what happened during Jesse's operation. It still eats away at me and whenever I recount it, I find myself breaking down. It was one of those instances, and there were several that year, where I felt powerless and unable to change the course of events, leading to the demise of another human being whose life was just beginning. By then I had years of experience and I had seen many tragedies in my career. This was the worst because I still think that it could have been prevented.

Things went relatively smoothly to start. The cannulas went in and Jesse's body was cooled. This was accomplished in several different ways, including packing ice around Jesse's head to protect his brain and running in cooled intravenous fluids. As well, he was lying on a special mattress through which either cool or warm water could be pumped. Full circulatory arrest occurred, and the cannulas were removed to give

Dr. Odim the access he needed to perform the repair. It is worth remembering that the cannula would be going back into the vessel (aorta) once it had been repaired.

Once the repair was completed, Jesse had been in TCA for forty-five minutes. He was now in danger of suffering neurological damage. Dr. Swartz, the anesthetist, became concerned and asked Dr. Odim if he was planning to repair the VSD before returning to "low-flow" bypass which was normally done. He replied that he was. Dr. Swartz pointed out that Jesse had been in TCA for forty-five minutes. Dr. Odim replied that he knew that and asked her if she was worried. She said she was and he replied "me too" and carried on. He was done in just over an hour. We all hoped there would be no neurological or tissue damage. In the end, TCA time was just over one hundred minutes.

About an hour after going back on bypass during the rewarming process, I had turned my back to the operative field and was attending to something on my table. I heard a gasp and as I turned back, I saw that the aortic cannula, which was millimeters away from the new repair on the aorta, had become dislodged.

Right away, I called out to the perfusionist, Mike, that the cannula was out. He stopped the pump immediately, otherwise it would have drained the baby of all his blood in seconds. This was a catastrophic event. It was something none of us had ever seen or experienced in our many years of working in the OR.

It is difficult to describe what happened next. Both Dr. Odim and Dr. Hancock tried to replace the cannula. They were disorganized and seemed panicky. They each made several attempts to put the cannula back into the aorta, grabbing the cannula from each other. They were arguing, and because the surgical field had become somewhat cluttered prior to this event, it was very difficult to reinsert the cannula. Dr. Odim seemed rough, jamming the cannula again and again into an area of the aorta, just millimeters from the repair he had completed. I remembered being horrified and confused as to how this could have happened.

The cannula was out for five to six minutes. This was calculated by the timers on the bypass machine and the anesthetist's monitors. It is indisputable. When it was finally replaced, Dr. Odim announced that he had destroyed the aortic repair. I don't think anything could have shocked or horrified me more. This meant going back on TCA, cooling Jesse down again and redoing the repair. His chances of survival were literally dropping by the minute.

The cooling process took some time, so I took a quick break and left the OR for a few minutes. As I walked down the hall, Mike came behind me, hot on my heels. I heard him call my name, and as I turned around to speak to him, he said "What the fuck happened in there, Carol?" Mike's a nice guy. I had never heard him raise his voice or curse. He was always calm, friendly and polite. This comment from him was indicative of how disturbed he was.

For the first time in my career, I cried, not for long and not out loud, but at that moment, I just couldn't hold it back. I have cried at home after some sad event, but I've always managed to keep it together at work. This was all so shocking and tragic. However, there wasn't time for crying, so I got a Diet Coke from the machine, went to the bathroom, and returned to my spot in the OR.

We went on to repair the damage that had been done to the aorta. When that was completed, Jesse was rewarmed but attempts to get his heart to beat again were futile. He was pronounced dead at 10:39 p.m. Around that time, Dr. Ward, one of the cardiologists, came into the OR. He was going to have to go and speak to the parents. Some of us over-heard Dr. Odim telling Dr. Ward it was best to tell the parents that Jesse could not be weaned off bypass and not to discuss the problem having to do with the destroyed repair.

It was another shock in an already horrible day. This is where I lost what little respect I had left for Dr. Odim. He was not going to tell Jesse's parents what really happened to their little boy! I heard this con-versation, as did the anesthetist and the cardiologist. I went home that night and made my notes about the case. I tried to relax in our hot tub. It had been a long and extremely stressful day. My legs were so achy and my mind was leaping around from one scenario to another, replaying all the events that had occurred that day. I thought that maybe I had it all wrong. It was so far from the norm for me that I had trouble believing what I had seen. Maybe, I didn't really understand what I had seen.

I was very tired. Still, I didn't sleep well that night. Maybe, maybe. Maybe…. Like anyone involved in a tragic event, my mind tried to come to terms with what I had seen. I needed to make some sense of it. It was like a movie running over and over in my brain. I felt like I was now part of some kind of coverup and that was disturbing.

What happened to Jesse Maguire was my worst nightmare come true. He was the eleventh child to die.

THERE IS A SAYING IN THE MEDICAL COMMUNITY: "If it isn't written down, it didn't happen." Meaning, everything that we do for our patient, every med we give, every treatment we perform, even what we say to our patient must be documented on the chart. If somehow we end up in court, that's the way it'll be looked at. So all disciplines are extremely careful about charting everything that goes on. In the OR, nurses have count sheets, a Nursing Record of Operation sheet, Input and Output sheets and so on. The perfusionists have their own record, where they document the pump run, cross-clamp times, blood gasses, TCA times, and everything else pertaining to going on and coming off bypass. Anesthesia has their Record of Anesthesia where they chart all the drugs given, vital signs and interventions that occur during the surgery. At the HSC, we had something called an IPN (Integrated Progress Notes) which means just that: anyone involved in the patient's care may document whatever they want on this part of the chart. Doctors, nurses, physio, pharmacists, social workers … anyone can and *must* chart.

Finally, surgeons have an Operative Report which they dictate, usually very soon after they complete the surgery. On it, they document exactly what they have done in detail from start to finish. Dr. Odim wrote nothing on his operative report or on the IPN about the accidental dislodgement of the aortic cannula and the destruction of the aortic repair. This complication was documented on the anesthesia record and on the perfusionist's record.

"First, do no harm." Words doctors are supposed to live by according to the Hippocratic Oath. This event created a great deal of anxiety, pain, and grief for me and almost everyone else who worked that day. It remains with me to this day. I think of Jesse often and with great sadness. I will never forget him.

After this case, several of us took our concerns again to our superiors. I did not go to work the following day. But the day after that, I went to see Isobel. She arranged for Irene and me to see Dr. Postl. Irene was devastated too. She had been there. She told Dr. Postl about an informal survey she had taken in which people "in the know" would never allow their child to be operated on in Winnipeg.

Dr. Postl asked us if we wanted the program stopped. We said no, we wanted these terrible events to stop. He seemed sympathetic. We told him that the problems that had occurred earlier in the year were still happening.

Dr. Postl contacted Dr. Blanchard and informed him of the conversations he had with the nurses and others, including a NICU doctor. One of the issues that was discussed was having Dr. Hamilton present. Nursing had talked about how much better things seemed to be when he was there. In the meantime, a devastated Dr. Swartz spoke with Dr. McNeill and Dr. Craig about her concerns about the way the operation had proceeded.

A meeting between Drs. Odim, Hamilton, Blanchard and Unruh took place in early December. They agreed that Dr. Hamilton should assist Dr. Odim in all neonatal and high-risk cases from that point on. This was written up in a memorandum from Dr. Blanchard to Dr. Postl and copied to Dr. Odim and Dr. Hamilton. Dr. Postl sent a copy to Isobel Boyle who showed it to me a day or so later. Seeing it made me feel marginally better.

The Wiseman Committee met on December 7 for the first time since October 17. No one was informed of the memorandum regarding Dr. Hamilton. Dr. Wiseman informed the committee that the cases from September, October, and November would be reviewed at the next meeting, which was scheduled for December 16.

The December 16 meeting never happened.

CHAPTER 16

ERIN PETKAU

There would be one more death before action would be taken. And that would be the death of Erin Petkau. I introduced Erin to you in the preface to this book. As we saw then, things began to go wrong for Erin shortly after she was born on December 17 in Morden. She had been a full-term baby but soon showed signs of blue spells and a heart murmur. That sent her to Winnipeg where she was diagnosed with long list of heart problems: a Tetralogy of Fallot (a condition which includes marked aortic override), a large VSD (a hole between the left and right ventricles), Right Ventricular Hypertrophy (heart muscle thickening), pulmonary valve stenosis (malformation which causes a blockage and malfunction of the valve), either an ASD or a Patent Foramen Ovale (a hole between the right and left atria which is a part of the fetal circulation), small pulmonary arteries, and a PDA (another part of the fetal circulation which closes shortly after birth).

Dr. Giddins performed an echocardiogram and concluded that as long as her PDA stayed open, Erin would be okay, but she would need a BT shunt soon. Dr. Odim was not available that weekend, so he was not part of these discussions.

A BT shunt was typically a "closed" procedure, meaning the patient would not be put on bypass. It usually took two to three hours to complete. We had done several of them over the years with Dr. Duncan, and apart from the general anxiety I felt by then with any case that Dr. Odim did, I didn't really feel any concern when I heard Erin was scheduled for the procedure.

On Monday morning when Erin's parents came to see her in the NICU, they were told to wait because she was being prepared for surgery. They were surprised as they had not been told that she would be going that day and they had yet to meet Dr. Odim. Around noon, Dr. Odim met with the Petkaus. He explained the proposed operation and that this was a way of assisting Erin until she was a bit older, at which point she would have a definitive repair. The purpose of the BT shunt was to reroute blood to Erin's lungs for the time being. Her anatomy at the time was such that once the PDA closed, her lungs would not be perfused with enough blood to sustain life. Erin's parents were not told of any of the ongoing problems within the cardiac program. Dr. Odim drew a picture of Erin's heart, explained a few things to them, and told them that the risk was low. Erin's mother said she was left with the impression that he was the best surgeon to do this operation.

During that night, Erin's extremities were cool and she was placed under a radiant heater. She was irritable but settled with sedation.

Erin went to the OR the next day at 12:40 p.m. Again, despite the directive from Drs. Blanchard and Unruh, Dr. Hamilton was not notified even though Erin was a neonate and in poor condition preoperatively therefore elevating her risk for surgery. Dr. Odim did not call Dr. Hamilton in to assist, though Dr. Hancock assisted as usual.

By this time, Dr. Hamilton had assisted on a couple of cases. He was definitely the better choice as an assistant because he was a cardiac surgeon. Dr. Hancock was a general surgeon. Dr. Hamilton would be more alert to problems and would have better knowledge and skills when it came to solving them. Dr. Hancock was a very good general surgeon, but her skill set lay elsewhere. Perhaps one of the problems Dr. Odim had was he felt embarrassed or intimidated by having another cardiac surgeon there with him. It is hard to say why he stuck with Dr. Hancock.

All I can say is I had lost confidence in Dr. Odim and Dr. Hancock by then and I felt better when Dr. Hamilton was there. He was a no-nonsense kind of guy and never seemed to lose his cool. However, Dr. Odim didn't call him, so he didn't know the case was on. Later he stated that he had been available that day and could have assisted had he been called. I really feel his presence would have given Erin a better chance. Two cardiac surgeons are surely better than one.

I WAS NOT PRESENT FOR THE ENTIRE PROCEDURE, but Erin's operation was one of the most distressing cases that took place that year. So many things went wrong. This was supposed to be a routine case. An operation that most of the cardiac team had seen done many times. We did not expect the disaster that it became.

At the end of the case, when the drapes were removed, it was noted that the cut-down that Dr. Odim had performed was bleeding profusely and that Erin had lost a lot of blood from that site. It had not been noticed because her tiny arm was under the drapes and not visible. This was very disturbing. Our cardiac surgeon had performed this simple procedure that I had seen residents do all the time. Dr. McNeill, the anesthetist, described it as extensive bleeding on top of everything else. By the end of the case, Erin had received approximately 800 to 900 milliliters of blood products. This was nearly three times her total blood volume of approximately 350 milliliters.

In the meantime, word had gotten to the NICU that Erin was not doing well. So Deb Armitage, one of the senior nurses, arranged for someone from Pastoral Care to come and see the parents. Shortly after Erin had been weaned from bypass, Dr. Giddins attended the OR and after a discussion with Dr. Odim, and not being overly concerned by all the problems, spoke to Erin's parents and told them that things were going fairly well. This was miles from reality. I don't know what planet he was living on that day or why he could be so cavalier. Apparently these two conflicting reports caused the Petkaus enormous pain.

Erin was transferred to the NICU in extremely unstable condition just after midnight. From there, it just got worse and worse. Once in the NICU, Erin could not maintain her blood pressure or oxygen levels and around 2 a.m., after discovering that the second shunt he had put in was clotted, Dr. Odim reopened her chest, flushed it and passed a catheter through it. Opening her chest caused more bleeding and trouble for this tiny girl. She continued to receive transfusions (three times her blood volume all over again in the NICU) and other resuscitative measures, but there wasn't much more to be done. As he had done with his earlier patients, Dr. Odim reopened her chest without anyone from the OR present. He did this with just a nurse from the NICU to assist him, a job totally out of her experience. No OR nurse or anesthetist was present. There is no way it would be safe for an OR nurse to care for a critically ill patient in an ICU with all the pumps, meds, ventilators, and so on, and no one should expect an ICU nurse to perform the duties of a trained OR nurse. This concept seemed to be lost on Dr. Odim. Again.

This was previously exemplified in the case of Jessica Ulimaumi several months prior. In that instance, Dr. Odim had to pinch off a bleeding vessel with his fingers which, as one can imagine, barely fit inside the chest of a small infant. He did not have the correct vascular clamps or sutures available either and Jessica bled out and died. Was there not a lesson to be learned there? Should we not learn from our mistakes? When he'd booked Jesse Maguire for surgery, he'd told the junior OR nurses working that weekend that they should be able to manage.

I have watched several other cardiac surgeons operate, both adult and pediatric, and they touched NOTHING except the structures they were actually working on. If they had to move something aside for a better view, they did it gently and carefully. Dr. Odim poked and prodded, pushed things aside and in my opinion did not seem to notice how much damage he was doing. What followed were the bleeding issues we all saw. He was so rough and the children suffered for it. I was not alone this opinion.

We weren't called back for Erin. I realize that by the time all this was happening we were all tired and asleep in our beds but any one of us would have returned to the hospital to assist and try to save Erin. She deserved the best care possible and, in my opinion, she did not receive it.

Barbara Petkau had no recollection of being told how desperately ill Erin was, so it wasn't until she was brought to the bedside that she realized her daughter was going to die.

Erin died at 7:50 a.m. December 21, 1994, in her mother's arms. Prior to that, according to one of the NICU nurses who was present at the time, Dr. Odim launched into a lengthy explanation about the many unforeseen problems Erin had. Further, a friend of mine heard him remark that they could always have another baby. Barbara Petkau was in her forties, and this was their first child. Later, I was told, Dr. Odim sat with his feet up on a desk, within earshot of the grieving parents and engaged in a "lively and apparently amusing," conversation with someone. Hopefully the Petkaus didn't notice. This was very disturbing to the staff.

When I arrived at work the following morning, one of the other nurses who had been there until the end of the surgery approached me and said, "we had quite a night!" She then told me all about it and what a terrible time they had had after I left. When Carol, who had also been at Erin's surgery, came at noon for her shift, she was told about Erin. She said she took a few minutes to collect herself by going into one of the operating rooms that wasn't being used at the time. Later, she told me all about the surgery as well. She was very upset. We both were.

She spoke to Karin Dixon and Isobel Boyle about Erin. I felt that since she was the one who had been there and because she was so upset, she should be the one to take this further. She had several conversations with Karin and Isobel, and Isobel spoke to Dr. Postl shortly after.

THIS WAS NEAR CHRISTMAS and so we all had some time off over the holidays. I spent the holidays wondering how I was going to cope with all the cases I knew were booked for January. I had a quick look at the schedule before I went on my Christmas break.

When I got back to work a few days after New Year's, I was in our locker room changing into my scrubs. Dr. Jo Swartz was there as well. I asked her what the plan was, to refresh my memory about the cases booked for the next few weeks. I said something like "what will we be doing in the next couple of weeks?" She said "Nothing."

"Nothing?" I asked.

She looked at me and said, "It's over."

I will never forget those words.

Erin was the last of Dr. Odim's patients to die.

PART THREE
THE AFTERMATH

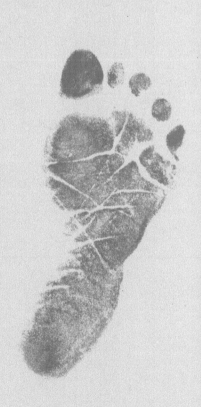

CHAPTER 17

WE HAVE QUESTIONS

Christmas holidays were over, and I had spent them in a very confused and desperate state. I didn't know what to do next as I seemed to have exhausted all my options. I had spoken to all the people in the "chain of command" and although my nursing superiors wanted to help, they seemed almost as powerless as I did.

I enjoyed my time with my family over Christmas, and I did not spend the entire time thinking about the last few cases, but as my vacation drew to an end, I started to dread my return. I wondered what awaited me. Did I want to continue working in the cardiac OR? I knew Dr. Odim disliked me, likely as much as I disliked him. He knew I didn't trust him, and at that point I didn't trust anyone making the decisions about the program anymore.

The Wiseman Committee hadn't addressed any of the real problems. It had concluded that issues had been resolved and that we were ready to take on all cases. Nothing could have been further from the truth. The team definitely lacked confidence in the surgeon and vice versa. Any way you looked at it, the whole thing was a mess. The Wiseman Committee seemed to me to have been a total failure.

There was no way I could or would stand up to a cardiac surgeon and tell him and the rest of the committee what I thought about his incompetence. I knew I had support, but I was a nurse. I was expected to come in and do my job. And I was happy to do that ninety percent of the time. But when the same things happened over and over again, horrifying me and my colleagues, I really didn't know who to go to anymore, or what to tell them. My options were limited to my nursing superiors.

Everybody knew what had happened and they were aware that it wasn't the norm. Some children died when they underwent cardiac surgery. I knew and understood that. I had seen it happen with other surgeons. It was how these twelve children died that was so disturbing. Botched repairs, excessive bleeding, and then, after all that, leaving the OR in unstable condition.

Other than extreme trauma cases, such as car accidents, stabbings, and gunshot wounds, I had never seen anyone bleed to death. In an OR, bleeding issues, no matter what the cause, were controlled. Things got dicey for sure, but no one panicked, there was always something that could be done. If it was a clotting problem, there were meds and blood products that could be given to deal with it. If it was a surgical bleed, a search for the bleeder was undertaken and it was located and dealt with. The OR was the place to deal with blood loss. Find it, deal with it, replace what blood was lost, stabilize the patient and then, and only then, transfer out. In one year, I had seen several children die from excessive blood loss, either in the OR or in the ICU shortly thereafter. Pacemakers didn't capture and pace properly, repairs had to be redone. It was the stuff of nightmares.

Daniel, Erin, Marietess, Erica, Jesse, Vinay were tragedies I found almost unbearable. All of the twelve deaths were. But Jesse Maguire was my worst nightmare come true. What happened to him was what I had feared would happen all year long. A totally botched repair, which had been destroyed by the surgeon himself. Those of us present in the OR had seen it happen.

It was all out there. As time went on, especially during the following year, I was repeatedly reminded that statistically the numbers weren't that bad. The mortality rate wasn't that high. However, the people who reminded me of this didn't take into account the fact that we had done low- or medium-risk cases for a good portion of the year. Even so, to me, it was the way the children died that was so troubling. Numbers, stats, learning curves and so on were often mentioned to me throughout the following months. Dr. Swartz told me that the program had been stopped. Temporarily? Permanently? At that time, I didn't know what was going to happen. I was soon going to find out.

The day after Erin Petkau died, Isobel Boyle met with Dr. Postl and advised him that she could not send nurses into the cardiac OR anymore. Since it was close to Christmas and she knew that the OR, PICU, and NICU staff would want time off, it was agreed not to book anymore elective cases until after the holidays.

THAT SAME DAY, Dr. Postl called a meeting with all the department heads involved with the program. This included Dr. Ullyot (pediatric anesthesia), Dr. Kesselman (PICU), Dr. Seshia (NICU), and Dr. Giddins (cardiology). Dr. Odim was not invited.

Dr. Giddins complained that he felt he could not participate because Dr. Odim was not there. Dr. Postl told him to sit down, and he did. Dr. Seshia, who was head of the department of neonatology, had already advised Dr. Postl that the neonatologists, being very disturbed by the deaths of their last two or three patients, especially the ones who had undergone what they considered relatively minor procedures, had lost confidence in the program. They felt that ethically they could no longer refer their patients to the program.

Dr. Postl told the group that he felt the program should be shut down. The others agreed. They would be sending future patients out. There were further discussions. Someone wondered what would happen if the department of surgery refused to accept this decision. Dr. Postl stated that he would advise them that patients would no longer be referred to the program.

After this meeting, Dr. Postl called Dr. Craig (department head of anesthesia) and Dr. Blanchard (department head of surgery) to let them know what was happening. Dr. Blanchard called Dr. Odim and let him know. Since it was coming up to Christmas, he advised him to take a vacation and get some rest.

Later, Dr. Odim would say he was surprised at the decision.

All these things happened in December, unbeknownst to me or any other nurses involved in the program. I felt shocked and disturbed that no one took it upon themselves to let me or my colleagues know. Again, the nurses were dismissed and made to feel that our views and feelings were unimportant. We were not considered during this decision-making time. They didn't have to call me directly, they could have had Karin or Isobel tell me, but I'm not even sure the nurse managers knew right away. It would have been nice to know that I didn't have to go back in January to the same hell I was in before Christmas. I wasn't surprised though. It was a decision made by the powers that be and I don't think they even realized that we should have been made aware too.

There were many things that I really didn't understand. I thought I knew how the system worked but there is what can be called a "code" between members of the medical profession. In other words, they rarely criticize each other. Our country is not as litigious as our neighbours to the south, perhaps because all medical expenses are covered by the government here, so there are no big bills to worry about, but all Canadian MDs are covered by malpractice insurance just the same. And lawsuits do happen from time to time. I was told that lawsuits having to do with children don't result in big payouts, since the dollar amounts are usually calculated based on loss of income as a result of the malpractice. But litigation was still a possibility, and the hospital's reputation could be damaged. I do not think that was paramount in the minds of the department heads at that time. Since patient referrals wouldn't be coming, there was no choice but to shut the program down, at least temporally. However, there was one more thing the heads of the departments thought should be done, and that was an external review. This meant bringing in people from outside the province to review the program and the cases, talk to the staff, and get an objective opinion about what had happened that year. Something that likely should have been done in May when the anesthetists withdrew their services.

Two doctors from Toronto Sick Kids Hospital (aka The Hospital for Sick Children), Dr. Bill Williams and Dr. Larry Roy, a cardiac surgeon and an anesthetist respectively, were contacted and they agreed to come to Winnipeg a few weeks later. They would be interviewing all the people involved, except the nurses. All the doctors were notified and told to prepare and submit their list of concerns. Once again, we were forgotten. Even though we had tried numerous times to bring our concerns to the attention of those in authority, initially we weren't considered important enough to be part of this process. I was angry but I was not surprised.

Dr. Ullyot from anesthesia submitted their concerns, which included case selection and the fact that the Wiseman Committee did not address their concerns in the end. She also stated that she felt it was important to involve the nurses and hear what we had to say.

Dr. Giddins talked about the review process and identified three phases: The first phase was the early part of the year, everyone becoming accustomed to the new surgeon and the first case selections. The second phase was in April to May, when the anesthetists withdrew from the program and the Wiseman Committee was formed. Finally, the third phase was the resumption of services, in the fall, and the taking of all comers.

Dr. Giddins was a junior cardiologist, trying to perform the duties of a senior one. Our city had had a senior pediatric cardiologist, Dr. George Collins, for years while Dr. Duncan was here. He had been a mentor for Dr. Duncan, who was just starting his career in 1986. Dr. Collins kept an eye on things, and I am sure there were times when he sent patients out because he felt the team wasn't ready for that particular case. He was known to cancel cases if he thought Dr. Duncan, who had been up all night, was too tired. He moved away shortly after Dr. Duncan left for the US. So Dr. Giddins was on his own until later in the year when Dr. Ward, also a junior cardiologist, joined him.

It was a recipe for disaster. A junior cardiologist lacking experience, maybe a bit starstruck by Dr. Odim's impressive twenty-five-page CV, and a junior cardiac surgeon, lacking experience, who seemed to have no insight into his own capabilities, and no one to mentor either of them. These two were left to their own devices for almost a year. There was no one there to say, "hold on, slow down, maybe we are biting off more than we can chew here." No one to take a breath, rethink, do some self-examination and ask, "are we ready to take this one on?" Were the benefits to the program being weighed against the benefits to the child?

Dr. Blanchard weighed in as well. He seemed to think that nursing and anesthesia blamed the surgeon unfairly for everything. He told the committee that he was unaware of any problems within the program until the anesthetists had withdrawn their services in May. Dr. Blanchard had tried to get Dr. Odim to work more closely with Dr. Hamilton but Dr. Odim seemed to have chosen not to follow this order. As Dr. Blanchard pointed out in his report to the Drs. William and Roy: "Unfortunately, Jonah has not always availed himself of this individual's assistance and support and one is left wondering why he did not do this?"

He ended his report with a list of several problems he identified within the program, including lack of mentorship, and issues with its surgeon who had poor communication skills, became flustered when things went wrong, showed problems with judgement when it came to case selection, and who had failed to spend time at the beginning of his time in Winnipeg with simulations and dry runs.

Nothing new there; we had been saying that for the past year.

Isobel Boyle was alerted to the fact that there would be an external review and upon discovering that nursing was not at the table, contacted Dr. Postl. He insisted that nursing be included. Without much notice, Irene Hinam, our anesthesia support nurse, and I were to prepare a list of concerns. The PICU and NICU nurses were not invited, so it fell upon Irene to talk to these nurses and document their concerns. We listed several. They were the same concerns we had been talking about all year. Poor communication, lack of preparation at the beginning of the program, excessive post-operative bleeding, lengthy procedures, long stays in the ICUs, more kids requiring pacemakers, problems with pacing, difficulties with ordering meds and treatments for patients in the PICU, low morale. Many of these ongoing problems had never been resolved. It seemed that the OR, PICU, and NICU department heads all had similar concerns.

To my knowledge, Dr. Odim had never answered any of the requests from nursing for information regarding patient care and protocols.

Communication was a big problem, not only with the staff but with parents. On one occasion, a parent asked for an interpreter to be called as she could not really understand what exactly Dr. Odim was telling her. He angrily dismissed this request saying that he was from a foreign country too, and if he could understand what was being said so could the parent. In a tertiary, core area hospital this attitude was unheard of. In any health care setting, informed consent was paramount. How could that happen when there was a language barrier? It was also disrespectful to the family of his patient, something I had never seen in all my years of working in a diverse institution like the HSC. Efforts were always made to accommodate all cultures and languages.

He had never found the time to meet with the nurses, even though he had been contacted several times by the different departments. I have never encountered this and still to this day can't understand why.

THERE HAVE BEEN MANY STUDIES investigating the conflicts between nurses and physicians and their differences in how they approach a problem.

Research has shown that doctors perceive less of a problem than nurses do because the nurse is with the patient more than the doctor. For example, there can be conflict about a doctor's order. Perhaps a nurse sees a patient in a lot of pain and feels that the pain medication should be increased. This may result in a conflict where the nurse feels he or she knows the patient better than the doctor and becomes frustrated when a doctor ignores these concerns.

A research article from the University of Missouri Center for Health Ethics referencing Barbara LeTourneau's article "Physicians and Nurses: Friends or Foes?" in the *Journal of Healthcare Management* identifies three main reasons for conflict between doctors and nurses:

1. The power imbalance between doctors and nurses whereby nurses are typically seen as being subservient to doctors who have years more education and training and who make the crucial decisions. This is despite the fact that today most nurses are graduates of a university with a Bachelor of Science in Nursing as well as taking post grad courses in their specialty.

2. Differing goals of medicine and nursing. In short, doctors focus on the disease and its treatment and nurses focus on treating the patient as a whole person.

3. Gender conflict between doctors, who have traditionally been men, and nurses, who have been mostly women. This is due to the old-fashioned notion that nurses as females should be subservient to the male doctor.

All these factors can cause tension and stress if a nurse feels under-valued, disrespected, intimidated and disempowered. I experienced all these feelings in 1994. I was "just a nurse" and deemed an overemotional female who couldn't handle the stress.

The most important conclusion from these studies is the same. Conflict between nurses and doctors can hurt the function of the team and result in poor communication, leading to poorer patient care and, in our situation, poor outcomes in the OR and ICUs. Therefore, senior management should take whatever steps are necessary to ensure that there is an environment in which destructive conflict is minimized and nurses are more empowered.

Further actions need to be taken to acknowledge the training and skills of nurses and changing the culture within health care to be more open and accepting of processes that catch mistakes early and to deal with mistakes as learning experiences.

Nurses take on a huge amount of responsibility and we strive to be accountable for our actions and the actions of our colleagues. The problem is we have very little power. In 1994, we could not get anyone with any power or authority to listen. We were dismissed again and again. So, in my opinion, we had to continue to participate in a program that was doing more harm than good.

IRENE AND I MET WITH THE TORONTO DOCTORS later in the day and outlined our concerns. I felt that by then, they had heard most of it already and that we weren't saying anything new. However, I hoped that now, with an outside perspective, someone would listen and something would finally go our way.

CHAPTER 18

EXTERNAL REVIEW

Dr. Williams and Dr. Roy were around for a day. They met with everyone, even the nurses in the end.

On February 3, 1995, they submitted their report to Dr. Blanchard. In their report were several findings and recommendations. They were careful. They stated that their report neither exonerated nor blamed the surgeon.

Their findings included questionable technical competence on the part of the surgeon. However, perhaps he had been judged unfairly because he tried to adopt our ways instead of insisting on his own. The program was poorly supported by the HSC administration right from the start and there was an absence of protocols for resolving disputes.

One of the things they recommended was amalgamating the program with Saskatoon's. Larger programs were known to have better morbidity and mortality rates and were more efficient because there would be two surgeons working together. Of course, if the program moved to Saskatoon all the problems would be solved in a single stroke, they said. If Winnipeg was chosen, new protocols would have to be established.

A 2012 abstract from a study from *The American Academy of Pediatrics* entitled "Association of Center Volume With Mortality and Complications in Pediatric Heart Surgery" examined how many children were operated on at a given centre along with their death statistics. More than 35,700 patients in sixty-eight centres were included. It found the more cases a surgical centre does, the better it gets and the lower the mortality rates are. There are many studies reviewing surgical outcomes, and they all show that higher patient volumes result in better stats.

Another recommendation was that if there was to be a program in Winnipeg all facets should be governed by three people: a doctor, a nurse administrator, and a hospital administrator. They also recommended that all patients go to one ICU post-operatively, that there should be fewer anesthetists involved in the program, and two more cardiologists should be hired. Finally, they stated that nurses should have a meaningful involvement in the decision-making process within the program.

On February 13, after receiving the report, Dr. Blanchard met with Dr. Postl, Dr. Craig, and Dr. Bill Lindsay, the new head of cardiac surgery who had just arrived in Winnipeg. They discussed the findings. Later, Dr. Craig advised Rod Thorfinnson, the CEO of the hospital, of the report's contents. A day or so later, a meeting was set up with the three department heads, Mr. Thorfinsson, his assistant, the HSC vice presidents, the deputy minister of health, and the assistant deputy minister of health. The Williams and Roy report was discussed. Initially all three department heads agreed that the program should continue, but without its present surgeon. When it came down to it, Dr. Odim wasn't going to be doing pediatric cardiac surgery in Winnipeg. Essentially, he was fired. I am not sure if this was because of a concern about public perception or if they realized finally that he wasn't up for the job. Or both. Perhaps someday he could be a competent surgeon, but in my opinion, while he had the knowledge and book smarts, he did not have the talent. He did not have the hands. He needed these attributes to be a successful surgeon. The department heads did not feel that a new program could or should be rebuilt around him. For now, the program would be suspended for at least a few months.

Mr. Thorfinnson stressed the need for a media release. There was a meeting with several people. I remember being there and Dr. Blanchard announcing that there would be a media release and someone saying to the group that they felt that it was a bad idea. There was a discussion, but in the end the decision was to go ahead with the release. The following day, on February 14, Valentine's Day, HSC released the press announcement:

> The Health Sciences Centre announced today that the Pediatric Cardiac Surgery Program will undergo an intensive six-month review to ensure that the best possible cardiac care service is available to young Manitobans and their families. This decision was made because patient outcomes have not achieved standards which the hospital hoped for when the program was re-introduced in February 1994.
>
> An external review of the Pediatric Cardiac Surgery Program was commissioned by the Health Sciences Centre in January 1995. The report of the external reviewers highlighted a number of areas in which the program could be improved, including staffing patterns, resource allocation and the meeting of outcome objectives. Fundamentally, the review questioned whether, in a population of about one million people, there are sufficient numbers of children requiring heart surgery to maintain the clinical expertise required.
>
> In the course of the next six months, the Health Sciences Centre will consider a variety of steps which might be taken to optimize the activities of the program. Such steps might include more formalized links with other centres where pediatric cardiac surgery is performed, reallocation of financial resources in support of the program and revisions to program staffing patterns.
>
> Patients requiring pediatric cardiac surgery have been transferred to Saskatoon or Toronto since Christmas 1994 and will continue to be transferred until the Centre's review has been completed. This practice, which has been routinely followed in the past, will ensure that Manitoba's children continue to have prompt access to the full spectrum of pediatric cardiac services during the six-month review period.

One big mistake was that no one thought to let the parents know about anything before the media release. They were completely in the dark and taken by surprise. Now they were finding out from the newspapers and on TV that the program that was supposed to help their children may have in fact either caused or contributed to their deaths. The pain and sense of betrayal they must have felt was incalculable. They were already dealing with the death of their child, and now this.

When the families read it, there was surely shock, enormous pain, and outrage. They demanded answers.

LATER THAT DAY, Dr. Blanchard met with Dr. Odim and advised him that the program was to be suspended and that if and when it resumed, he would not be the surgeon. He told Dr. Odim to resign, an alternative to being fired I guess, and to start looking for a new position elsewhere. Dr. Odim told him he would have to think about that. In fact, later that evening he called Dr. Blanchard and told him he would not resign. He stayed on for a period of time, doing adult cardiac surgery.

Despite Dr. Odim's extensive Ivy League education and training and his lengthy CV—facts that were pointed out to me frequently throughout that year—he had managed to keep his first job for just one year. When he finally left, he was given a "golden handshake." I don't know how much gold was involved. However much it was, it was worth it to me.

CHAPTER 19

"WE NEED ANSWERS"

Now the families knew. They knew the program was fraught with problems, that there had been more than one attempt to either slow or shut it down. They found out that there were several members of the team who had voiced concerns about what was happening. They were horrified and angry. Their children were gone. Nothing could change that. And no one had told them about the problems, the slowdown in May and the concerns about the way many of these children died. No one had offered them the opportunity to send their child out of province for their surgery, even when Dr. Giddins and Dr. Odim had been asked about this option by more than one parent. They were told that the Winnipeg team could handle it.

One parent was quoted in the local newspaper stating that the nurses should have done more, that we should have told them before we took their child into the OR. This was a terrible thing for us to read. I remember Irene and I talking about this and how broken we both felt. We tried to believe that this mother had spoken out of anger and frustration and that hopefully, if she was ever to hear our side of the story, she would not feel that way anymore. But it hurt. Deeply. We couldn't help but wonder if perhaps she was right. Even though we knew by then that we could not have stopped the program.

The parents wanted, needed, and deserved answers.

They began phoning the hospital, the doctors, the media, trying to get answers. Several of the parents met with Dr. Giddins, Dr. Odim, Lois Hawkins, and staff from the Patient Relations Office. They soon learned their questions were never going to be adequately answered. They were frustrated and angry. No one could tell them why the program was shut down. There was no mention of surgical incompetence or bad judgement.

Dr. Giddins and Dr. Odim told them they had no idea this was going to occur. One parent described them as being nervous and evasive during their meeting. Both had "sweat marks" in their armpit areas, she recalled.

These parents must have been shocked and horrified by the level of deception and evasiveness they encountered. Parents had entrusted their child's life to these doctors. Some parents from outside the city, especially those from more remote Northern communities, were unable to get any information. Attempts to call the doctors and other staff proved to be unsuccessful.

Some parents declined to meet with the staff. Others found the meetings to be unsatisfactory, a "run around" was how one parent put it. No real explanations were given and expressions of sympathy weren't enough.

The parents of Vinay Goyal, Aric Baumann, Marietess Capili, Ashton Feakes, and Jesse Maguire met several times with either Dr. Odim, Dr. Ward, Dr. Giddins, and other people from HSC.

I was back at work, doing my normal routine, general surgery, ENT, orthopedic, and plastic surgery cases and trying not to worry about what was happening behind the scenes. All of us were relieved that the program had been halted, but we still didn't know what was going to happen next. I knew that Dr. Odim was still operating on adults, and I would see the perfusionists from time to time in the hospital hallways. We didn't have much to say to each other.

We were reading about these parents in the newspaper. Article after article. Day after day. The media had gotten hold of a story and were not letting it go. Every day there was another horrible take on what these parents had gone through.

It enraged and almost destroyed me. I felt like screaming. I cried. As an OR nurse I had very little contact with the parents, and towards the end of 1994, I had stopped taking the children from their parents and into the OR. Now I also felt a huge burden of guilt settling on me.

I wondered if I would ever get the chance to tell my side of the story about what I had witnessed that year. If so, I was going to tell them everything, talk about all the things that I had seen in that OR that year. I wasn't going to minimize anything. I was terrified that I wouldn't be able to control my emotions and I mentioned to someone that I was so scared I would "lose it" and cry. That, I thought, would damage my credibility. I'd look like that over-emotional female who couldn't take the stress of my job. Exactly what the doctors seemed to think I was. Someone told me that crying wasn't necessarily a weakness and that anyone who had experienced what we had would have to be made of stone if they didn't feel sad and cry for these children and their families. In the OR I never cried, even when I felt like I was on the verge, in some very difficult situations like dealing with an abusive surgeon. I was always able to keep it together. Now I wasn't so sure. I had so many mixed feelings. However, the nurses still hadn't heard anything about what was going to be done to satisfy the parents.

We waited.

ACCORDING TO MANITOBA LAW, all pediatric deaths are reported to the Office of the Chief Medical Examiner (OCME). Autopsies are ordered on a case-by-case basis. When an autopsy is ordered by the office of the medical examiner, the Manitoba Fatal Inquiries Act states that a report must be completed and submitted within thirty days. Unfortunately, this didn't happen, and as much as the pathologists were encouraged to finish their reports, the workload was too great. At that time there were only two pediatric pathologists. It was usually impossible to make the deadline.

The manner of deaths are categorized. This is different from the cause of death. There are five categories of manner of death. They are:

1. Natural
2. Accident
3. Suicide
4. Homicide
5. Undetermined

All death certificates must state both a cause and manner of death. An example of this could be:

Cause of Death: Blunt force trauma to the head, due to a fall from a height.

Manner of Death: Accidental

In this example an investigation into the death done by the police and/or the medical examiner investigator would conclude that this person wasn't pushed (homicide) or didn't jump out of a ten-storey window on his own (suicide). If the investigation was unable to determine the circumstances of the death, the manner of death might be ruled undetermined or pending further investigation.

While many, but not all, natural deaths are reported to the OCME for various reasons, all the other categories MUST, by law, be reported. For instance, if someone dies within twenty-four hours of admission to a health care facility, or if they die within ten days of a surgical procedure, they are reportable under the Fatal Inquiries Act. They are looked at by the OCME and if there are no concerns—for example if someone with a history of severe heart disease, who has had two or three heart attacks in the past, comes into the ER clearly having had another—the case is handed back to the attending doctor who will then sign it off with a cause and manner of death. No autopsy is necessary. There are many other reasons a death may be reported, including a case where the cause of death is unknown.

The twelve children who died at the HSC's pediatric cardiac centre were reportable for two reasons: they were children and most of them died within ten days of their surgical procedure. Next of kin could request a copy of the autopsy report. They could choose a summary report with the cause of death but few other details, or the complete report, which was very detailed and went through everything, organ by organ, system by system, all test results and findings.

When I left nursing in 1997, I took a job with the OCME and it was part of my job to inform the next of kin that there would be an autopsy if ordered and that they were entitled to a report. Unfortunately, there was a backlog, and it was often months before the families received them. I always called the families of my cases and gave them the cause of death over the phone within a couple of days, but the actual written report took months.

When a child dies during or shortly after surgery, the medical examiner is authorized to order an autopsy. Sometimes, if the parents request no autopsy be done, their wishes can be considered on the condition that they understand that this is the one and only chance to find out what happened. If there are criminal proceedings or if the death is suspicious, an autopsy is always performed. However, in any situation, the ME still has the authority to order an autopsy without the parents' consent if he feels it is necessary. In these cases, two families, early in the year, requested that an autopsy not be done, perhaps for cultural or religious reasons. Their wishes were honoured. In one other case, an autopsy was not performed due to a communication problem.

Unbelievably, even though all twelve cases were reported to them and reports were written, the medical examiner was not made aware of what was happening in the pediatric cardiac surgery program in 1994. No trend was noted, likely because several different investigators were dealing with the cases. No information about the slowdown in May, the Wiseman Committee, or the Williams and Roy review was made available to the medical examiner. Not even the shutdown at the end of the year. None of it. The Chief Medical Examiner (CME) later stated that he read about these things in the newspaper just like the parents and the general public. Upon learning about all of the above, the CME contacted the parents and informed them that there would be an investigation into the deaths of their children. As well, he contacted Dr. Walter Duncan, a pediatric cardiologist from British Columbia, and requested he conduct another review into the deaths. Upon receipt of Dr. Duncan's report, Dr. Peter Markesteyn, the CME, called an inquest into the deaths of the twelve children on March 5, 1995.

There was also a committee of three pediatric surgeons who reviewed the surgical deaths of these twelve children. This committee consisted of Dr. Ray Postuma (a pediatric general surgeon), Dr. Wiseman and, unbelievably, Dr. Odim. So the review of the twelve cardiac deaths was being done by their surgeon. When Dr. Wiseman was questioned about the ethics of this situation, he agreed that it was problematic, but they dealt with it by asking "challenging" questions and trying to get "objective" answers. "You recognize your own failings and put them on the table, and it works." He said most people (not all) were willing to take responsibility and say, "I screwed up." Maybe in a perfect world. Ours wasn't.

I wondered what Dr. Odim said about his cases. I couldn't imagine him saying he had "screwed up." In my experience, his response to difficulty or criticism was placing the blame on others. Me, for not having the right suture or instrument available, the fact that there were two ICUs caring for these patients, the anesthetists for several reasons, the perfusionists for not giving him the correct cannula, his assistant Dr. Hancock for not clamping a line when taking Jessica off ECMO. And on and on. There did not seem to be any accountability on his part. I don't think his ego could handle it. Later in an interview with the *L.A. Times*, Dr. Odim described those of us who questioned or critiqued him as "hornets buzzing around him." Again, it seemed to me he tried to portray himself as a victim. To him we were just a colossal pain in the ass, getting in the way of his career.

In March 1995, Dr. Odim distributed an eight-page open letter stating that he felt his colleagues "deserved to have an account of the program's activities." It contained statistical information about the cases he had done. He received several letters of support from other physicians and from the families of some of his surviving patients as he continued to operate on adults throughout the following months.

CHAPTER 20

THE PEDIATRIC CARDIAC INQUEST

The Pediatric Cardiac Inquest began in December 1995. It ran almost three years, until the fall of 1998, making it the longest-running inquest in Canadian history. More than eighty people testified over the 285 days of hearings. Close to 50,000 pages of evidence were produced and hundreds of documents exceeding 10,000 pages were submitted as exhibits.

The need for an inquest is determined by the Chief Medical Examiner as stipulated in the Fatality Inquiry Act. He may call an inquest if he feels the general public will benefit from the information made public during such a hearing. The inquest process cannot determine culpability with respect to the deaths. No blame is laid. It is a fact-finding process. A provincial judge presides over it and makes recommendations at the end to ensure that whatever took place never happens again.

This was a big deal. No one knew who would have standing at the inquest. In these proceedings, all those who participated must attain standing. They must have a legitimate reason to give evidence for it to be granted by the presiding judge.

As nurses, we felt we definitely had something to say and so we waited for someone to contact us. There were several groups who had standing right off the top. The doctors: Odim, Hancock, Hamilton, Giddins, Wiseman, Blanchard, Unruh, Kesselman, Seshia, Ward and several others had lawyers who were hired and paid for by their medical malpractice insurer. The hospital had its own set of lawyers, and since the nurses were hospital employees, we were told we would be represented by them. Early on, we were told that we likely wouldn't be called. Once more we were treated as unimportant participants in this whole thing. Our evidence was not required, at least by the lawyers acting for the hospital. Even though we had been there on the frontline throughout.

The government was represented by one lawyer, the anesthetists by two more, and the families by several. Some of the families banded together and were represented by one lawyer, and a few had their own. Shortly after the proceedings got underway, the government provided the families' lawyers with funds to pay the fees. Most families, if not all, could not have afforded the legal costs. That became clear early on.

Two of the lawyers were crown attorneys, Don Slough and Christina Kopynsky, whose job was to organize the witnesses and interview everyone prior to their day(s) in court. They would start the process in court with their witness examination. They would get the background information and set things up for the judge so he could understand who was who, who did what, what their duties were, etcetera.

There were two high-profile criminal defense lawyers, Saul Simmonds and Hymie Weinstein, who represented some of the families and the anesthetists respectively. So the courtroom was full.

The inquest was presided over by Judge Murray Sinclair.

Not long after the inquest began, I was contacted by Isobel Boyle and informed that the hospital's lawyers wanted to meet with the nurses from the OR. Carol Dupuis, Irene Hinam, and I met with two "suits" in a room in the basement of the Children's Hospital The lawyers were polite and attentive initially. I was wondering what the point of the meeting was going to be. I wondered if they were going to tell us that we were going to have to testify and that they would look out for us. Actually, what they said in the end was that they didn't think they would need us to testify. Basically, it was kind of a "don't you ladies worry about a thing, we don't think we will need to hear from you." We were shocked.

Carol, Irene, and I looked at each other and then we said, "but we have these." At that point we shoved our notes forward, the ones we had made after several of the botched repairs and terrifying events that had occurred over that year. The ones I had sat up at night typing on my home computer after seeing what I can never, ever un-see. The look on their faces was priceless. They took our notes and had a cursory look at them. The tone of the meeting changed instantly. There was definitely a cooler attitude that replaced the paternal and patronizing demeanor we had just seen. I swear the temperature in the room dropped by a couple of degrees. The meeting was over, and we were told we would hear from them soon.

A few days later, Isobel Boyle came up to the OR. She met with two or three of us. Her face was white and she looked extremely upset. She said that the lawyers representing the hospital felt they could not act for the nurses because there might be conflict of interest. It seemed our notes made the doctors and the hospital look bad. Turns out, we had something to say!

Who would look after our interests now? None of us could afford to hire a lawyer for this. We were nurses for goodness sake! We were terrified. We had no idea what to do. At that point we were on our own.

I remember thinking about my family. Both my husband and I had good jobs, but there was no way we could afford a huge legal bill. I felt guilty that I was now bringing financial problems to our marriage. How would I pay for this? *Take out a loan? A second mortgage? Ask my mother for some money?* It kept me up at night.

CHAPTER 21

OFF TO COURT

So our employer ditched us. Left us high and dry without representation. At one point a couple of the other nurses and I attended one of the first inquest hearings. Judge Sinclair spotted us in the gallery and was aware that we were nurses involved in the case. He commented to an investigator from the Medical Examiner's office who was there that he thought nursing should have separate standing. She passed on the message to us at a break. At that point we really didn't know what that meant. We had no idea about how this all worked. We wondered, what exactly did "standing" mean, legally? We found out later that it meant the we had a legal right to be there, that we could give evidence pertaining to the issue at hand. In the meantime, I wondered who would help us if and when we were called to give evidence.

We set up a meeting with a lawyer from the Manitoba Nurses Union (MNU). By then the union was aware of the upcoming inquest and even though they were sympathetic to the situation we were in, they couldn't help us because our legal problems had nothing to do with our nursing practice specifically. The MNU dealt with workplace and contract issues mostly. Our case wasn't about nursing issues. As well, the Canadian

Nurses Protective Society (CNPS), to whom we paid fees through our membership in the Manitoba Association of Registered Nurses (MARN, now known as the College of Registered Nurses of Manitoba), which was our regulatory body, did not represent nurses involved in inquests. If we were going to court for some malpractice issue or misconduct, or if we were being sued by a patient, we could have had our representation paid for by the CNPS. This was a completely different situation.

It was Diana Davidson Dick who came to our rescue. She was the director of the MARN at that time. She had come from Ontario and while she was working there, the case involving Susan Nelles had taken place. Susan Nelles was an RN who worked in a pediatric ICU at the Hospital for Sick Children in Toronto. At the time she was there, several unexplained infant deaths occurred in the NICU between July 1980 and March 1981. It was determined that at least one child had died of an overdose of Digoxin, a commonly used cardiac drug. Three nurses were at the centre of the investigation and one of them, Susan Nelles, was charged with four murders. The case was eventually dismissed because she was not present when another child, not part of the indictment, died. An inquiry later determined that the deaths could not be proven to be homicides, no conspiracy between the nurses was ever proven either, the charge just wasn't credible, as claimed by the head of pediatrics at the time. Basically, there was a lack of solid evidence. It has never been prosecuted, and according to the police, it is officially an unsolved murder case. A second suspect, also a nurse, was not prosecuted.

Many people in the medical community, especially nursing, felt that Susan and some of her colleagues had been scapegoated. Nurses are at the bedside and have direct access to a patient 24/7. However, it doesn't follow that they should be suspected of a crime because of this. But that's what happened. I think Diana was afraid that something like that was going to happen again. Somehow, some or all of the blame for what had happened would land in the laps of the nurses.

Diana Davidson Dick called on the MARN to release some emergency funding for legal representation for us. Two lawyers were hired: Michael Richards and Brian Meronek. We met with them in their office on a

Saturday afternoon shortly after they were hired. They seemed competent and sympathetic to our situation. We discussed the salient nursing issues and I described some of the situations I had found myself in.

Not long after that, I was summoned to a meeting with the board of directors of the Health Sciences Centre. Michael Richards accompanied me to the meeting in a boardroom with a lot of scary people seated around a big table. They all seemed to be staring at me when I walked in, and I felt a bit like an animal in a zoo. Intentionally intimidating, I thought. I wasn't sure what the purpose of this meeting was, but I assumed that it was an attempt by the board to understand things from my perspective as an OR nurse. And so I started to tell them about myself, my experience, my job description, and Dr. Odim.

Mr. Harold Buchwald, a board member, asked me why I had made notes about some of the events that occurred in the OR. I replied that I felt that at some point there might be a lawsuit and that I should keep notes in case I needed to refresh my memory. I also described a conversation with Dr. Odim where he told me not to insult the intelligence of the nurses in the PICU when I suggested that an OR nurse should be present when certain problems that required a surgical procedure arose in the unit. An example being the need to reopen a chest in the ICUs. The PICU nurses knew me and were grateful when I or another OR nurse showed up and assisted in these situations that were clearly out of their scope of practice. I also told Mr. Buchwald that I and the majority of the staff who worked with Dr. Odim felt that the program was unsafe and would never let him near our children. I mentioned that I had been made to feel that I was over-emotional and that I was overreacting to this situation and described a conversation I had with a male coworker who told me that he would "get the boys from the General (the adult OR) to come over and do the work if I couldn't handle it."

Finally, when asked about the Wiseman Committee meetings, I stated that they did not accomplish anything and that I often felt uncomfortable there. Michael Richards interjected from time to time and seemed to be looking after my best interests. The meeting lasted about an hour, and I never heard much about it after that.

Twenty-some years later, in 2019, I was honoured to participate in a presentation at the "Jubilee Lecture" that the School of Nursing of the Winnipeg General Hospital (now the Health Sciences Centre) Alumni Association puts on every year. That year was my 50th Reunion. We were the "Jubilee Class." Four of my classmates, including me, spoke about our varied nursing careers. We wanted to illustrate how diverse a nursing career can be. One classmate spoke about her career as a parish nurse, one spoke about her experiences in Saudi Arabia, one spoke about how, after she retired, she and her therapy dog visited people in the hospital (she even brought Daisy, her collie, to the presentation). Finally, I spoke about my job with the department of justice as a death investigator for the Office of the Chief Medical Examiner.

We were a diverse group and our presentation was very well received. There was a lunch after, and I was approached by an alumnus by the name of Margaret Steele who had been at that long-ago meeting with the HSC board of directors. She told me that she wanted to apologize to me for what happened that day. She felt that I was put in a very unfair situation. I was surprised, very touched, and grateful for this. It meant a lot.

After the meeting with the board, we continued to wait, wondering if we were to make an appearance at the inquest. In the meantime, as I read the newspaper accounts of what was happening, I felt more and more uneasy.

Then, a month or so after Mr. Richards and Mr. Meronek were hired, MARN fired them. I had no knowledge of what had led up to this decision, but I was shocked and frightened when I got the call from someone at MARN telling me to come to their offices a few days later and meet our new legal counsel. The only explanation I received was that these lawyers seemed to be the wrong fit for us and that perhaps they were too much a part of the "old boys' club."

A few days later, I walked into Diana's office and was introduced to Colleen Suche and Bill Gange, our new team. They were a married couple at that time and were very pleasant and not at all intimidating. I remember looking at Colleen, who is petite and very pretty, and thinking she might not be tough enough to handle this. Boy, was I wrong! Colleen was up to speed very quickly and made me and the other nurses feel safe and comfortable right away. She was the mother of three young boys, her best friend was a nurse, and she seemed to understand how distressing this situation was. None of us had any legal experience, no idea what to expect, we were entirely out of our element and in their hands. This turned out to be the best decision Diana could have made. We soon grew to love both Colleen and Bill. They are terrific lawyers and human beings. Whenever we went to their offices, we were treated like family by the other lawyers and admin staff who we got to know really well over the next couple of years. Because of this relationship I will refer to them by their first names as that is what we did back then. All the other lawyers will be referred to by their last names.

We could call anytime if we had concerns. They were always patient and available. I remember Colleen giving me her phone number at the lake. I told her I didn't want it because I didn't want to bother her on the weekends, but she insisted that I could call her there too. She was the best thing that happened to us.

Sometime around then, we were told that the nurses involved could expect to be called as witnesses. We were told that this would happen sooner rather than later. So we started to prepare. Each of us spent hours in Colleen's office going over patient charts, minutes of the Wiseman Committee meetings, documents, memos, etcetera. I was to go first. We didn't know when exactly; we would have to wait for the call.

In the meantime, the parents who chose to participate appeared in court. Their evidence was heartbreaking. It made predictable headlines in the media.

The parents of Jessica Ulimaumi, Gary Caribou, and Erin Petkau were not directly contacted by the hospital to talk to doctors and Patient Services, according to their evidence later in court. Months later, one of the crown attorneys travelled to Inuvik to speak with the Ulimaumi family. Gary Caribou's mother stated that she found out about what had happened by reading it in the newspaper and that her husband tried unsuccessfully to telephone Dr. Odim. Lois Hawkins testified that she spoke to a representative from family services in Lynn Lake about Gary Caribou in an attempt to set up a meeting with the parents. She was told that the family was "all right."

Gary Caribou's mother, Charlotte, testified that when her son was first diagnosed and she was told by Dr. Giddins that he needed surgery sooner rather than later, she was not informed that there was no surgeon in Winnipeg at that time. She was not offered the option of sending Gary to Saskatoon or Toronto. "I thought the doctors knew what they were doing," she said. "They gave me papers to sign and the way they talked; I believed them—that they could save my boy."

She had travelled the 1,079 kilometres from Lynn Lake to Winnipeg on the night bus so she could speak at the inquest about her son. She brought photos of Gary to show the judge, some taken at home and the last one of her holding him wrapped in a white blanket to cover his surgical wounds, in the hospital, after he died. His eyes were closed and he looked like he was sleeping.

Charlotte asked Judge Sinclair to make changes so that doctors are more accountable to parents. Because English wasn't her first language, she had trouble understanding the doctors she spoke to, so most of the decisions for Gary were made by them. Though HSC has a department dedicated to providing culturally appropriate support and resources (including translators) for Indigenous patients, it wasn't clear whether anyone had connected Charlotte with Aboriginal Services.

Daniel Terziski's mother Danica spoke at the inquest about offering to fly in a surgeon, Dr. Christo Tchervenkov, chief of cardiovascular surgery at Montreal Children's Hospital, at their own expense. Dr. Giddins had become upset at this suggestion, threw his pen down on the table, and said it was unnecessary. She was told by Dr. Odim that Daniel's chances were 50/50 and that the Winnipeg team was capable. I'm sure they felt intimidated by Dr. Giddins' behaviour. I had seen a demonstration of it on more than one occasion. She had no real choice but to believe and trust them. She asked Judge Sinclair to recommend the doctors be more open and honest with the parents. She spoke about feeling abandoned by the system.

Alyssa Still's mother, Donna, felt uneasy about the surgery the night before it was scheduled. She and her mother, who had travelled to Winnipeg to be with her and Alyssa, worried about the possibility that Alyssa might have pneumonia and when they approached Dr. Giddins and Lois Hawkins, a nurse from the Variety Heart Centre, about their concerns. Donna and her mother described them as being "short" with them. They told Donna that the surgery had to be done and she was made to feel that she had no choice but to go along with this decision. They were not told until their arrival in Winnipeg to testify at the inquest about an X-ray taken two days before surgery that showed that Alyssa's pneumonia was slightly worse than an X-ray taken a day before. Donna stated that had she known about the pneumonia, she would never have allowed the surgery to proceed. "We felt totally lied to from day one," Donna told the inquest. Alyssa's grandmother stated, "We went from sticking right by the doctors to hating them." They were told that the success rate for Alyssa's surgery was around ninety-five percent and that Dr. Odim had worked in Montreal and Boston. They thought he was an experienced surgeon. Donna suggested Manitoba should set up a hot-line like Calgary's where the public could phone in and get information about a doctor's training and experience.

Linde Feakes, Ashton's mother, said "I know I can never get my son back, but in his honour I'm going to keep on fighting to find out what went wrong and that it never happens again."

Aric Baumann's mother, Deanna, testified that they were never told of the problems within the program that year. Aric died of an undiagnosed congenital defect which was not picked up until weeks after his surgery. He never left the PICU after his operation. She described Aric's last moments as the family stood around his bed. As she held him, she noticed that his oxygen saturations were dropping. She knew that Aric was dying. "I told him, it's okay, it's time to rest. No more fighting. Then he was gone." She sobbed openly in court as she said these words. Aric died in his grandmother's arms. He was the seventh child to die.

Judith Bichel, Erica's mother, testified that she was never informed that the surgical team had only been working together for a few months, that the anesthetists had threatened to boycott the surgeries and called for a review in May 1994, that high-risk surgeries had been suspended from May until September, or that Dr. Odim had performed only one similar procedure and that that child had died. She was told by Dr. Odim that Erica's chances were 50/50. She'd been informed by Dr. Ward that Erica's chances were 30/70 against survival. Dr. Ward told her that surgeons usually give higher rates of survival.

Dr. Giddins testified that he approved the decision to attempt the Norwood and that he felt no compunction to discuss it with, or get a consensus from, anesthesia or nursing. He stated that he felt that the team was much better "integrated" after the Wiseman Committee meetings and that they should go ahead the surgery. This to me, was another sign of the unrealistic view Dr. Giddins had. He seemed to have no clue about interpersonal relationships, being part of a team in the OR where every member had an important role to play. Judge Sinclair seemed to feel the same way. He commented in his report that Dr. Giddins' statement "seemed out of touch considering the animosity and the difficulties expressed at those meetings."

I was shocked and dismayed when I learned that we were going to attempt another Norwood, in light of what had happened to Daniel. Daniel was a bit bigger and older than Erica and although he was a very sick little baby, he wasn't as "catastrophically unwell" as Erica. However, because of her critical condition transferring her to another city would have been very dangerous. She was just too ill.

Dr. Ward was asked why he didn't present that option to the parents, and he stated that because he was fairly new to the program, having not worked there very long, he deferred the decision to do the operation to Drs. Giddins and Odim.

Dr. Odim was questioned about the decision to perform this procedure, given a letter he had written to Dr. Blanchard less than a week before. In this letter he had indicated his dissatisfaction with the program. He complained that there had been a concerted effort by the department of anesthesia to derail the efforts to build a pediatric cardiac program. He was asked if there was a contradiction between the decision to operate on Erica and the feelings he expressed in the letter written on September 26. A portion of the letter read: "In addition, I must confess that the basic trust that develops between surgeon and anesthetist as they care for a child in the operating theatre has certainly eroded [sic] by this conduct. One can only hope that this state of affairs is remediable and not irrevocable."

He replied that Norwoods had been discussed at the Wiseman Committee meetings and he felt that there was no indication that we should not be embarking on the procedure as a last-ditch attempt. In the end, there seemed no other option other than to go ahead with the surgery in Winnipeg. To this day, I feel that despite the risks in transferring Erica to another centre, her chances of survival would have been greater had she gone to Edmonton or Toronto. I don't know what they would have been, but I believe her chances in Winnipeg with Dr. Odim were zero. As a parent, I understand that Erica's mother and father were willing to try anything to save their daughter.

Shalynn Piller's mother Sharon stated that her daughter's death was "God's will." She is the only parent who testified that she found no fault with Dr. Odim and Dr. Giddins. She spoke about how she and her husband had received a call from HSC at midnight after the operation, and that Shalynn died about six hours later. She was told the success rate for an operation like her daughter's was around ninety-two percent. She asked about transferring her daughter out and was told that surgery could be handled in Winnipeg. She knew nothing about the moratorium or reviews. However, she still expressed gratitude for what the doctors had tried to do.

Barbara Petkau was told by Dr. Odim that Erin's operation was low risk. Again, like the other parents, the Petkaus had no knowledge of the problems within the program. Erin was the last of the twelve children to die.

The parents' testimony took several days, then one day while I was at work, I was told to pick up the phone in the theatre I was in. It was Colleen, telling me that I was to appear at the inquest the next day.

I MET COLLEEN AND BILL AT THEIR OFFICE the next morning and we walked the two or three blocks to the building where the court was set up. Because this case was so big and there were so many moving parts, an entire floor of an office building had been made available for the staff. The judge, the crown attorneys, and their support staff all worked there.

A few weeks earlier, I had met with Christina and Don, the two crown attorneys who were handling the case. They met with every witness (as far as I know) prior to their appearance in court. Colleen was there with me, and we went through all my concerns, the cases involving the twelve deceased children as well as some other incidents that had occurred during surgery performed on some of the surviving kids. They even took me down to the courtroom, so I could see where I would be giving evidence. This was reassuring, to actually have an idea of what was coming, where I'd sit, where Colleen and Bill would be. So this, along with my preparation by Colleen and Bill, made me feel reasonably confident.

I was very, very naive. At the time, I was confident because I believed without a doubt that I was right in my assessment of Dr. Odim and what happened that year. However, being right didn't necessarily mean that everyone in court was going to agree and be nice to me. There is always someone else whose perspective is different from mine. So Dr. Odim's lawyers and the hospital lawyers were waiting to have a go at me. They were paid to find holes in my story, flaws in my character, anything to discredit me in the eyes of the court. They put their personal feelings aside and did the job they were paid to do. They took instructions from their clients. I understood this. However, it was hard not to wonder what they really thought of Dr. Odim.

I can remember only bits and pieces of my twelve days in that courtroom. Most of what follows is what I remember and from reviewing the transcripts of my testimony.

And so, my first day in court came and went with Christina Kopynsky questioning me about my experience. How long had I been a nurse? How long had I worked in an OR? How many surgeons I had worked with over the years? How many were cardiac surgeons? We began setting the stage.

We talked about Dr. Duncan, the years we'd worked together, the team that had been built, his departure to the USA and the hiring of Dr. Odim. Then we started to talk about what happened in the OR. What had happened to those twelve little humans? We went through them one by one.

I told my story, what I had seen and experienced. All from my perspective as a nurse. The excitement and anticipation around the first case. The immediate disappointment in the way Dr. Odim treated me and my nursing colleagues. Finally, how it become clear that there was a problem with surgical skill and competence. And with his lack of insight.

It started with little things, like where to place the equipment, what went where, not being familiar with our ways of doing things despite several invitations to meet with nursing and being offered a dry run. The problems escalated to difficulties with cannulation, bleeding issues, botched repairs, and poor communication, and ended with the tragic patient outcomes.

From time to time, I would look around at all the lawyers sitting at their tables and see horror and shock on their faces. Many were staring down at their laptop or legal pad. Sometimes I could hear the parents in the gallery crying. I could look over at the gallery and on most days, see some of my friends, my husband, and my sister. All there to support me. Also, members of the press, writing furiously as I spoke. Ms. Kopynsky took about a day and a half, and when she was finished, Colleen asked me a few more questions, filling in some blanks. Then the cross-examination began.

Mr. Hymie Weinstein was next. He was a very well-known criminal defense lawyer and was acting for the anesthetists. I felt relatively comfortable answering his questions. He was an experienced and talented lawyer, thoughtful but direct in his techniques. We went over several issues, but I didn't feel particularly uncomfortable because I knew his clients were pretty much on the same page as far as how things had unfolded that year. He took about a day to complete his cross-examination.

Now, it was the hospital lawyer's turn. This is where things got unpleasant. I felt uneasy and wondered what they were going to try to pull on me. They represented the hospital, and if things had gone as planned, they would have been our lawyers too. They had dumped us, out of fear or concern for the reputation of the Health Sciences Centre. The hospital had left us to fend for ourselves. When this all began, I was saddened and disappointed by this. However, at the end of it I knew that they had inadvertently done nursing a huge favour. We had a lot to say and with the backing of our own lawyers, we were permitted to tell our side of the story without being muzzled, as I am sure we would have been had the HSC been looking after our interests. Since we were nurses, not lawyers, we would have been compelled to follow the wishes of our employer, who paid the lawyers. We would have been told what to say and how to say it. The focus would have been to protect the doctors and the reputation of the hospital. As nurses, we would have been the ones to take the fall for a lot of what happened. No one would have stood up for us the way Colleen Suche and Bill Gange did.

Their main focus, as it turned out, was the Wiseman Committee and what happened at those meetings. We went through them all in detail. At one point, when Mr. Richard Hanlon was hammering away on something recorded in the minutes, I finally had enough. I had already admitted I didn't remember a lot of what was discussed at the meetings. I was pressed to answer questions and if I had difficulty to refer to Dr. Wiseman's minutes. Well, those were sporadic at best. At one point I interrupted Mr. Hanlon and asked if I could say something. I told him, as I had told him on several other occasions, that I didn't remember the conversation he was talking about.

Then I let him have it. I told him that as I read Dr. Wiseman's minutes, I often wondered if we had been at the same meeting. Nowhere was there any mention of Dr. Odim taking shots at me after I had left one of the meetings early, even though Dr. Wiseman told me about it later. Nor was there any mention of my challenging Dr. Odim at the next meeting about his comments regarding me, or of Mike Maas defending me when Dr. Odim complained about a needle driver he was waiting for. There was no documentation of Carol Dupuis mentioning that nursing did not feel comfortable taking on more difficult cases, or of the resulting flack she took from Drs. Odim and Giddins at that meeting. Judge Sinclair commented on my point and added that he had some questions about the minutes too and hopefully when it was Dr. Wiseman's turn to give evidence, he would enlighten the court.

Mr. Hanlon brushed off my statements and continued on picking away at my recollections of the events at the meetings. This lawyer was taking instructions from my employer and trying to discredit me. It was hard to take. I asked myself if I should resign from my job at the Health Sciences Centre. I didn't need this, and I didn't deserve it. I had worked hard; my performance evaluations, done every year, were excellent. Why were they trying to make me look bad now? It was exhausting and soul crushing.

Once I was being cross examined, I was on my own. Colleen and Bill really couldn't prepare me any further. Now and then, I would glance over at Colleen, Bill, and Diana sitting at a table across the room. Diana would straighten up in her chair, reminding me to sit up straight. Colleen told me that sometimes I would do this on my own. I'd kind of gather myself and sit up straighter when the going got tough. She said she enjoyed watching me do this. She knew I wasn't defeated.

It took the hospital lawyers about three days to complete their cross examination and then it was the lawyers for Dr. Odim and Dr. Hancock's turn to take a crack at me. I expected this was going to be rough, and I was right. Mr. Raymond Flett was an older man, and his partner was Mr. Tyler Kochanski. Mr. Flett did all of the talking and Mr. Kochanski stood beside him the whole time and stared at me, sometimes smirking at my responses. This was a new strategy. It was disconcerting at first, but I soon realized that this was a ploy to intimidate me. Two against one. It worked for the first day or so, until I figured it out. Mr. Flett and I spent five or six days together, back and forth, me answering his questions over and over. Sometimes the same question worded differently would be asked, I suppose in an attempt to trip me up.

Toward the end of those days, I felt that I could not take much more and told Colleen that if it didn't stop soon, I was going to lose it and tell the two of them to go fuck themselves. Colleen assured me that this would be a bad idea.

One thing that Mr. Flett seemed interested in was Dr. Odim's request that I scrub for him for every case the first six months or so. Dr. Odim told me he thought I was good at my job and wanted me there all the time. I told him that I couldn't do that because other nurses needed the experience. I might get sick or be away for some reason and I should not be the only one who knew the ropes. I told him that my boss Karin Dixon would not be in favour of this either, as it was crucial that more than one nurse be familiar with Dr. Odim's cases.

Also, I had had more than one conversation with Dr. Odim about the fact that I worked part-time. Four days a week, eighty percent of a full-time position. His comments to me about this implied that he didn't feel that I was really committed to my job because I wasn't working full-time. I explained that I had a young child and that I liked that one day off to book appointments and so on and that I always worked the days where cardiac cases were scheduled. However, he seemed to take some delight in making me feel bad about it. I don't think he realized that many of us want some sort of work-life balance. Work is important, but our family life is too, especially when our kids are young.

Somehow, despite these explanations, it seemed that Mr. Flett was implying that perhaps things might have gone better if I had scrubbed for all the cases, thereby trying to assign some of the blame on my refusal to do that. Again, disturbing and soul crushing. I would go home and wonder about it. *Maybe I should have agreed to do as Dr. Odim had asked?*

My instructions from Judge Sinclair were that I could not discuss any of what went on in court with anyone while I was under oath. The days I was in court were spread out and not consecutive. Scheduling all the lawyers and witnesses took some finagling. So I was left with my own thoughts and doubts for several weeks. I managed to talk myself out of these doubts as the days passed. But it made me uneasy and ultimately very angry that Mr. Flett was trying to divert some of the blame away from his client. Was I going to become a scapegoat too? Would the judge see through that? So on and on and round and round we went. I thought it would never end.

While I was giving evidence in court in 1996, I received many cards and messages of support. One card was especially meaningful to me. It had a message of support from a nursing colleague and on the front of the card was that famous photo from the sixties of a young person putting a flower into the barrel of a soldier's gun at a protest. Again, so many years later, it resonated with me, and I took it with me to court and placed it on the table I was sitting at. I would glance at it from time to time during some of the more difficult cross examinations and it calmed me and gave me strength. After a day or so, Mr. Flett noticed it. He objected to my having this card and asked that I put it away. Judge Sinclair instructed me to remove it, which I did immediately. I remember thinking that this card and the resulting objection to it were kind of like the event depicted in the photo: the smaller and weaker person making a statement despite being placed in danger. I wasn't in physical danger of course, no guns were pointed at me, but my professional and personal reputation were being assaulted. The weapons were words, not guns, but they were designed to wound me just the same.

Sometime during all this, Margaret Feakes, the grandmother of Ashton Feakes, left a message with Diana. Part of it read:

> I feel for Carol and would like her to know that the parents are really, really behind her. We have had prayers for her for a couple of Sundays to give her strength. We will continue to pray for her while she is on the stand. If you let her know we feel she is doing a very, very courageous thing. We thank her. So please tell her that we really are praying for her and we will continue to do this and please tell her to stand firm because there are a lot of people behind her and we do appreciate her.
> —Margaret Feakes. Ashton's Gramma

There are no words to describe how I felt when I read this. To this day it makes me cry. It meant so much. It really helped and gave me strength. I remember seeing Margaret in the courtroom frequently. I don't think we ever spoke, but I was aware of her presence there and after seeing her message, I did feel stronger and better for it.

Finally, Mr. Flett completed his cross examination. Next came several lawyers for the families. Mr. Brent Stewart was the first to go. He represented Erin Petkau's parents and he focused on a couple of things. He mentioned the Health Sciences Nursing Award that I had been given in 1995. We talked about how I came to receive this award. We spoke about Dr. Wiseman and the meetings. We spoke about how I felt about Dr. Odim and the toll working with him took on me and some of the other nurses. Finally, at the end of his examination, he told me that his clients, Mr. and Mrs. Petkau wanted to thank me and the other nurses for our courage in trying to protect the interests of babies like Erin, despite what he imagined were adverse consequences to our professional career and livelihood. His voice broke a little when he said that last part. The room was silent for a few seconds. I thanked him for those words. They meant a lot and I have never forgotten them. Here was an example of how difficult it must have been for all these lawyers to sit and listen to the evidence day after day. Grace comes in all forms, and I have always tried to remember that despite the pain and anguish the parents went through, they were willing to forgive.

Next came Mr. Martin Corne, representing Jesse Maguire's parents. He was a little harder on me. He focused on the events surrounding Jesse's disastrous operation and death. He asked me many detailed questions about what had happened and how I felt that day. I told him that Jesse's death has always been one that greatly affected me. It was my worst nightmare come true. During that year, I had been fearful of some disastrous event in the OR. All the deaths were horrible to witness, and Jesse's death was one that completely devastated me. I was there with Jesse when he died. I saw it all: the bleeding, the struggle to reinsert the aortic cannula, the destruction of the newly completed repair, and the final decision to stop all treatment and let Jesse go. It was the stuff of my nightmares for years after.

Mr. Corne then asked me the question I had been asked before, why I didn't come forward sooner to warn the parents, why I didn't tell the parents to "take your baby and run" as I had stated at some point that I wanted to do. Again, I explained my reasons and concerns about doing that. The following response is taken verbatim from the court transcripts:

> Well, first of all, when I see these parents, we are literally at the door of the operating room. They have gone through all the pre-op teaching, they have gone through the stress of preparing themselves for this particular event, and I can't imagine anything could be more stressful for a parent than something like this. I could sort of paint a picture of what it would be like if I had gone out to this parent and said, "stop, you can't do this, take your baby and run or whatever." I wouldn't have said it like that, but just don't take this child. I don't want to take your child in.
>
> What would have happened then would have been all hell would have broken out. They would have called Dr. Odim, they would have called Dr. Wiseman probably, called the director of nursing up. There would have been this big group of people come to this, wherever we were, waiting room or wherever. I would have been very upset by then, probably crying. There would have been Dr. Odim, and Dr. Giddins, and whomever, calm, cool and collected. I would have looked like an emotional, almost crazy person. You know, they would have just thought, they would have talked to the parents, they would have said, maybe this nurse is just overreacting, maybe she is over emotional.
>
> As a parent, I think it would have depended on the parents. Would they have listened? Maybe they would have backed off, maybe they would have said let's wait another day and rethink this. Maybe they would have listened to Dr. Odim, listened to Dr. Giddins, whom they knew and had met several times before, and don't forget, they are just meeting me for the first time at that point. I don't think it would have done any good. I think perhaps I could have saved that one child, and I still think about that from time

to time. But there would have been more kids come in, the next kid—I would have been out of there. I would not have had that job anymore. I would have been out of there. The program would not have stopped, and there would have been more kids come in the next day or the next week. And nothing good would have come out of that.

I didn't kid myself. I was good at my job, but no one is indispensable.

Colleen later praised my response. She said I painted a clear picture of exactly what would have happened if I had done that. Although nurses had a lot of knowledge and expertise, along with a great deal of responsibility, it is expected that our concerns be limited to our professional duties, and we should not critique those "above" us.

Mr. Saul Simmonds was next. He represented several of the families. He was one of the well-known criminal defense lawyers at the inquest. Although this was not a criminal case, he was good at getting to the root of the problem and for fighting for his clients. He was pleasant and focused on my relationship with Dr. Odim and his treatment of the nurses. His questions prompted a long discussion between the judge and several lawyers about whether to go "In Camera." This told me that they knew what was coming. In Camera evidence is heard only by the clients (meaning the parents of the twelve children), the judge, the lawyers, and the witness (me). It was decided to do this, so the courtroom was cleared of everyone else. I was then asked about some of the sexist remarks and insults Dr. Odim had said to me and other female staff over the year. I laid it all out for them. It was difficult and embarrassing to repeat what he had said to me, but I felt that although I didn't report it at the time (as I should have done), it felt good to tell someone that day. I cannot discuss the comments he made. However, a few years later, a reporter for a national newspaper found out and it was published. No one knows who told him, he didn't have to reveal his source. It certainly wasn't me.

Colleen and Ms. Kopynsky had a few more questions for me and then, after twelve long and grueling days on the witness stand, I got my chance to say some final words to the judge. I had been told I would have this chance at the end, so I had prepared something and I read it to the court. I asked the judge to listen to the nurses who would follow me into the courtroom, and I apologized to the families. Then, I was done.

Initially, the plan had been for me to go and meet with some of the other nurses who would be testifying later on. That day, I felt I couldn't do it. I just wanted to go home. As I walked out of the courtroom and into the adjoining office, I broke down for the first time. I was so exhausted. I just sat down and cried. I still feel that I let my nursing colleagues down that day, but I was just not capable of talking anymore. And I didn't want them to see me break down right before they were to go to court.

I feel that I did okay. I learned a lot. The biggest lesson was that no matter how confident I was about right and wrong, there would always be someone who would try to discredit me and pick holes in my evidence. I had been told that an inquest was a fact-finding exercise and not a trial. No one was going to jail or being sued. Yet, I felt I was attacked by Dr. Odim's lawyers and by the lawyers for my employer, the Health Sciences Centre. I understood the former's motivation, but not the latter's. I had always assumed that my employer would protect or even thank me for bringing these issues to their attention. *Wasn't safe and competent care the most important thing that a health care institution is to provide? Why was no one watching Dr. Odim?* No one seemed to care about what was happening at Children's Hospital, and that was hard to understand. That was a valuable lesson for me and any nurse to learn. We were all experienced and respected by our surgical counterparts—as long as we knew our place.

With my time in court behind me, I tried to support the other nurses who followed me in there as much as I could. Carol Dupuis followed me. Irene Hinam, Karin Dixon, Isobel Boyle, Joan Borton, Donna Feser and Deb Armitage, Colleen Kiesman, Mary Jane Wasney all appeared later in 1996 or 1997. Every one of them did an excellent job of getting the nursing perspective across. The perfusionists, the anesthetists, and several other doctors gave evidence, including Dr. Giddins and Dr. Odim, who spent seventeen and twenty-five days on the stand respectively.

Now we waited.

CHAPTER 22

FINDINGS AND RECOMMENDATIONS

The inquest carried on long after we nurses appeared. There were two hundred and eighty-five days of hearings and the proceedings ended in December 1998, with more than eighty witnesses called.

We had a lot of media attention. *Chatelaine Magazine* did a piece on us, and several nursing journals wrote articles. Newspapers had articles highlighting some of the issues. CBC's *The Fifth Estate* did a show, as did other news outlets. A crew from England came over to do a piece about it. Before they decided to come to Winnipeg, I met them in Boston for a day or so, I guess so they could check me out. A made-for-TV movie called *Open Heart* was produced and shown on the CBC. The main character was loosely based on me and I participated as a medical consultant. From time to time, the producer would call me to run a scenario by me. Of course, it was highly dramatized and the disappointing thing for me and others was my character being portrayed as having a drinking problem. Was this another way of downplaying nurses' legitimacy? I didn't spend much time worrying about it though.

The people in my life knew I didn't drink much and I didn't care what the rest of the world thought.

At first, after we had all testified, my colleagues and I agreed to do speaking engagements, mostly to groups of nurses (OR nurses, orthopedic nurses, student nurses), and at several conferences. We travelled around the country. Usually it was Irene, Joan, Deb, Donna, me, and occasionally Colleen, our lawyer. My portion of the presentation was about what happened in the operating room. I would talk about the difficulties we had, the technical problems Dr. Odim had, what occurred with some of the children. We had a PowerPoint presentation titled *Any Nurse, Anywhere,* which included photos of some of the deceased children. The title of the presentation was meant as a warning for nurses. Even if you have years of experience, even if you are well liked and respected professionally, even if you are friends with your medical coworkers, you may pay a heavy price if you dare criticize or even voice a mild concern about the competence of a doctor. Irene, Joan, Donna, and Deb spoke about events in the PICU, the NICU, and the Variety Heart Centre. Colleen would talk about the inquest and the legal issues.

Getting through these presentation was difficult. I could never make it past the description of what happened to Jesse Maguire without having to stop and collect myself. My voice would break, I would pause, get it together, and go on. I would see people wiping their eyes as my colleagues and I spoke about what happened that year and its aftermath. Many nurses approached us afterwards to thank us for speaking out. They often told us about similar events that they had witnessed.

We received standing ovations every time.

This went on for a few years. Sometimes we did these presentations as a group, sometimes I went alone. At one conference in Montreal where I went alone, I gave my presentation and, as usual, it was well received. Later that day, I participated in a panel discussion, the topic of which I have since forgotten. There was a doctor on this panel and at one point when he was referring to my presentation, he started his remarks with words to the effect of "if what Ms. Youngson said actually happened ..." The implication was that he really didn't believe my story, or that I was exaggerating the facts. This happened before the report was released. I guess as a physician, he didn't feel that a nurse could possibly get it right when commenting on a doctor's competency. I remember being shocked that he would say this with me sitting right there on the same stage, but I said nothing. After the discussion, I was approached by a couple of nurses who knew him, who told me not to pay him any attention. That he was an arrogant so and so. But this was a prevailing attitude among the medical community. Over the years, during and after the inquest, I heard from only two doctors I had worked with. One called me at home to tell me he supported me and the other approached me at work to say he thought we had done the right thing. Another doctor who saw me as a patient commented that she thought what we had done was very brave and admirable.

Most of the nurses I worked with were very supportive. Certainly Karin and Isobel were behind us all the way. However, I soon hit a point where instead of it getting easier as time went on, it began to become more difficult to do the presentations. So I began to turn down the invitations. I finally had to stop talking about it altogether.

And life went back to normal. I had my family, my home and my work to keep me busy. I tried to put it all behind me. Time went by and we all waited for the inquest report. We knew it would take some time. There were more than eighty witnesses, over fifty thousand pages of transcripts and ten thousand pages of submitted documents for Judge Sinclair to go through.

Then, in 1997, my mother died. Her death hit me hard. I was heartbroken. Six months earlier she had moved from Melville, Saskatchewan to Winnipeg to be closer to me, my husband, and her grandson. Following some abdominal surgery, she declined rapidly and we lost her.

The day before she died, we had spent hours in the HSC Emergency Room. She had been complaining of abdominal pain. After spending most of the night and day in the ER, I decided to go home for a while. I needed to get some sleep and see my family.

The next morning, I went over to see her as soon as I got to work. She was sleeping, but I wanted to talk to her and see how her night was. Her nurse told me not to waken her. I walked back to the OR. As soon as I got there, I got a call from the ER doctor. She told me my mother seemed to be doing well but they still didn't have a handle on what was causing her abdominal pain. They would keep her until they figured it out.

Despite the doctor's words, I knew I needed to get back to see my mom right away. I felt like she was calling me back. I ran through the hospital tunnels to get there. As soon as I got to the ER, I heard some-one say, "There she is." A very gentle nurse took me to a small waiting area where we could be alone. She told me my mom was now in the resuscitation room and things didn't look good. She had collapsed as they tried to get her out of bed. She was now intubated and on several drugs, including Levophed, which I knew was a last-ditch resuscitation drug. I went into the resus room and stayed with my mom during her last moments on this earth. By then my husband and a friend were there, as well as her attending doctor, a surgeon, ironically Dr. Blanchard, who was kind and caring in his treatment of my mom and me. I remember crying uncontrollably and his hand on my back, which was oddly com-forting, but tears kept coming from a deeper place of grief I didn't know existed. Like a dam had finally broken.

For three years prior to my mother's death, I had been involved in a tragedy that never seemed to end. I didn't realize how incredibly sad I was because of what I had witnessed and experienced as a cardiac OR nurse. I went home and, except for about three months in 2010, I never worked as a nurse again.

I stayed home for over a year, rested and regrouped and during that time I came to the conclusion that I needed to do something different. I applied for a job with the Manitoba Department of Justice as a medi-cal examiner investigator (MEI). Something totally different. I was one of over one hundred applicants for the position. They hired two of us. I started in August 1998. I know I wasn't the smartest or most experi-enced candidate. I am pretty sure I got the job because of all the media coverage. I was well-known in the medical/legal community. Initially I wasn't sure if I'd made the right decision. However, it turned out to be the best job I ever had. I loved it, I was good at it, and I worked there for about seventeen years.

In November 2000, there was a buzz in the air that the report might be coming out any day. And sure enough, one Friday, Colleen and the other lawyers received their copies and were advised that it would be released to the public on Monday morning. All parties were informed not to speak to anyone or reveal its contents. That Sunday, Colleen called me. When I picked up she said "Ask me if I'm smiling." I asked "Are you smiling?" She replied "Yes!"

Judge Sinclair's report contained many findings and recommendations. It had been the longest inquest in Canadian history, lasting over three years. The report was long and thorough. After discussing all the findings and recommendations in detail he concluded with this:

> The evidence suggests that some of the children need not have died…The evidence from these proceedings suggests that the deaths of Jessica Ulimaumi, Vinay Goyal, Marietess Capili, Jesse Maguire and Erin Petkau involved some form of mismanagement, surgical error or misadventure and were all at least possibly preventable or preventable. The operations on Daniel Terziski and Erica Bichel involved procedures that were probably outside the ability of the surgeon and the team to attempt and ought not have been done in this province. The operation on Shalynn Piller was outside the permitted parameters applicable to the team at the time of the operation and ought not to have been done in this province.
>
> The deaths of Gary Caribou, Alyssa Still and Ashton Feakes are still surrounded by more questions than answers. Only the death of Aric Baumann from a fatal and untreatable disease has been acceptably explained.

Judge Sinclair wrote a massive report: 516 pages, including three appendices. It can be accessed online by anyone at pediatriccardiacinquest.mb.ca. In his findings and recommendations, he wrote about each individual child as well as general findings and recommendations regarding the program itself.

Reading the report was both heartbreaking and gratifying. The heartbreak stemmed from the knowledge that several of the deaths were preventable. I believe the chances of survival for these children were limited because they were operated on in Winnipeg. They should have been sent out. It was obvious that Dr. Odim was not skilled or proficient enough to perform some or all of these operations. The lack of experience and insight into his own capabilities was stunning. To me, attempting a Norwood, arguably one of the most complex and high-risk operations performed to date on a neonate was completely irresponsible. Even the most experienced surgeon would hesitate in a situation where he is the new and only guy in town. It still confounds me that the more senior physicians, either directly or peripherally involved in the care of these children, did not question the wisdom of embarking on a case like that in Winnipeg, so early in the career of this surgeon. No one did. No one said *"Wait a minute, let's take a breath. It is too soon!"* Both the surgeon and the cardiologist were in over their heads. It was obvious to the nurses who were working alongside them. We were right and that was the gratifying part.

Finally Judge Sinclair ended his report with this:

> From all the facts and evidence that have been uncovered, there is one that stands out. The deaths of these children were not the result of any failing on the part of the parents. There was nothing that they did that they ought not to have done. There was nothing that they did not do that they should have done. Faced with the situation that each of them saw, they did what they believed was best for their child and they acted on the basis of the best information they were able to obtain.

The day I read this I cried. Then I sent an email to Judge Sinclair. Two words. "Thank you."

CHAPTER 23

FALLOUT FROM THE FINDINGS

I was the first of our group to go to court. A few days before I testified, the other nurses got together and bought me a small heart-shaped pin. The heart had a jagged break running through the middle of it with a bandaid on it. It was made out of pewter. I wore it proudly. As time went on, we all got one. Everyone chipped in and we all wore our little broken heart pins whenever we got together.

THE BROKEN HEARTS CLUB
Members:

Irene Hinam: Anesthesia nurse
Carol McGilton (now Dupuis): OR nurse
Carol Youngson: OR nurse
Donna Feser: PICU nurse
Deb Armitage: NICU nurse
Joan Borton: VHC nurse

Although we had many other supporters, we were the core group. We had been there and seen it all. However, we did not stay silent as nurses in the past had been directed. I still have my little pin, so many years later.

From time to time we went out for dinner together. We even had a favourite booth at The Keg, a steakhouse in downtown Winnipeg. We would discuss the events and our experiences in court after we had all completed our time there. We supported each other and it was great to have this feeling that there were colleagues who understood exactly what we were going through. Later, we bought one of the pins for Colleen as well, and she joined our group when she could. Colleen and I have been friends ever since.

Colleen is now Madam Justice Colleen Suche, Court of King's Bench. When she became a judge, she invited us to the ceremony and the party afterwards. We were honoured and thrilled for her.

As the years went by, we all went in different directions, career-wise, and we lost touch. I haven't seen Donna or Deb (who passed away recently) for years. Irene and I run into each other from time to time and Joan also passed away a few years ago.

ONCE IN A WHILE, something wonderful happens. I mentioned in a previous chapter how affirming it was to run into Daniel's mom, Danica Terziski, and Marietess's dad, Ben Capili, and receiving encouraging words in a voicemail from Ashton's grandma, Margaret Feakes, while I was in court.

A couple of years ago, I met some friends for lunch at a local restaurant. All of us were retired nurses. I was the last to arrive and while I was getting settled, our waitress approached and one of my friends spoke to her saying "this is the nurse we were telling you about." Before I had arrived, the waitress had been talking to my friends. She had been operated on as an infant in another city in 1994. She had been sent away for cardiac surgery during the spring or summer when our program had slowed down for the review. We chatted for a couple of minutes. As she walked away, she turned to me and said, "Thank you for saving my life." *Did I actually play a part in that?* I was unable to reply, I could only smile.

I have thought of that conversation often. I don't think she realized what her words meant to me, but each time something like that happens, some of the pain falls away. I have no idea who she is, but her words are another reason I write this book. Years before, around the time my name had appeared in the media a few times, I saw a letter-to-the-editor published in the *Winnipeg Free Press*, written by a mother of a child who would have come for heart surgery about the time the program was shut down. She thanked me as well, for saving her child's life. I still have that clipping in a little picture frame in my home.

Finally, in early 2023, my sister Kathy called me from Mesa, Arizona where she and her husband were wintering. She told me that she had run into a woman there, and as usual, the first question was "Where are you from?" Kathy said she was from Canada and the woman replied she was too, Winnipeg in fact. When Kathy mentioned she was from Saskatoon, this woman related a story about the one and only time her family had travelled to Saskatoon. Their infant daughter had required open-heart surgery in 1995 and the parents were told they had to go to Saskatoon as the program in Winnipeg had been shut down. Kathy replied that she knew all about it as her sister had been one of the nurses involved. This woman knew the story and became very excited and stated that she wanted to thank me and the other nurses for saving her daughter's life. We have emailed back and forth, and she and her husband have expressed their gratitude to me and the other nurses involved. Their daughter is doing well. These things are important and never leave me. I like to think some kids were saved during the months we sent patients out and after the program was shut down for good.

CAROL AND IRENE CONTINUED TO NURSE for several more years, though both eventually left Children's OR.

Judge Sinclair became Senator Sinclair and later went on to chair the Truth and Reconciliation Commission, which dealt with the horrific generational damage resulting from the abuse Indigenous children endured at Canada's Residential Schools.

Over the next few years, both Dr. Odim and Dr. Giddins left for positions in the United States. Initially, Dr. Odim went to Atlanta, Georgia. However, his temporary permit was not renewed because he failed to mention on the application that there were legal proceedings involving him in Manitoba. When a reporter from Winnipeg contacted the person who had hired Dr. Odim, they had no idea. Apparently, according to the article the reporter wrote, there is a specific question on the application form about whether the candidate was involved in legal issues to which Dr. Odim had answered "no." After leaving Georgia, he then moved on to California. Dr. Giddins took a job in northeastern United States.

At the time of this writing, Dr. Odim is a senior medical and scientific officer in Bethesda, Maryland. Dr. Giddins is a pediatric cardiologist in Vermont. Dr. Wiseman retired in October 2022. At this time, Dr. Hancock still practices at Children's. Dr. Postl moved on to bigger and better things within the Winnipeg Regional Health Authority.

PART FOUR
COULD IT HAPPEN AGAIN?

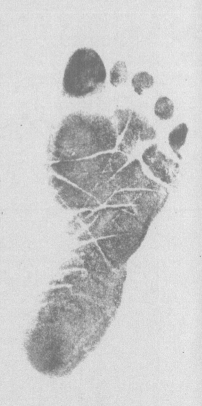

CHAPTER 24

... AND NOW

On the day Judge Sinclair's report was released in 2000, a committee appointed by the new NDP government to assess progress on his recommendations met for the first time. The committee, headed by University of Manitoba political science professor Paul Thomas, was given one year to assess progress on Judge Sinclair's thirty-nine recommendations. In May 2001, *The Report of the Review and Implementation Committee for the Manitoba Paediatric Cardiac Surgery Inquest* was released. It assessed the merits and practicality of the recommendations. But most importantly, the report concluded "a repeat of the tragic events of 1994, which led to the deaths of 12 infants, is unlikely given the changes that have been implemented throughout the health care system."

Manitoba's health care system had begun the first wave of reform to "better manage health care and to provide better service." In 1997, eleven regional health care authorities were reduced to five. Organizations like the Health Sciences Centre that had been "stand-alone silos" were amalgamated with other hospitals and services under the control of the Winnipeg Regional Health Authority (WRHA). The HSC became an operating division of the WRHA in 2001. So there was a whole new layer of governance keeping a watchful eye on the hospital.

Transformation of the system continued in 2018 with a new centralized organization called Shared Health that governed clinical and business services. The goal was to reduce duplication of management and administrative functions, while ensuring each region was able to provide health care according to a provincial clinical services plan and to make sure services provided centrally were coordinated and consistent. The HSC became a Shared Health facility in 2019.

The first report of the Review and Implementation Committee in 2001 noted that while Judge Sinclair could not make recommendations designed to change the health care system in general, many lessons were learned during the inquest. One of these was that while there is no shortage of laws, rules, codes, guidelines oversight bodies, etcetera, there was a great need for cultural change. For real change to happen, the system needed to shift from a legalistic individualistic and blaming approach to a cultural, collective and learning approach to accountability. The report noted there was a need to restore trust in the health care system.

The causes of the deaths of the twelve children were both individual and systemic. Families were understandably angry that the individuals they believed responsible for the deaths of their children did not pay the price for their errors or inactions. Beyond the conduct of the individuals, there were serious systemic failures involved in the events of 1994.

Adding to the families' pain was the realization the program had problems that were not shared with them and only by hearing about it later in the media were they made aware that the program was suspended. This added to their deep sense of grief and betrayal. Both Judge Sinclair's report and the Review Committee's report recognized that nothing could erase these feelings

Recognizing all this, the Review Committee made a commitment to the families that the primary aim of their recommendations would be to prevent a repeat of anything like the tragic events of 1994. Some of their recommendations to support the protection of patient and families and to ensure that they are treated with the respect and dignity they deserve were stricter policies around informed consent and improved physician-patient communication, the establishment of protocol for both patients and employees to lodge complaints or concerns about the treatment of patients, and to have them dealt with proactively and in a timely manner. Many of these were in implemented, or in the process of being implemented in the years following the publication of the report.

Even so, it is important to keep in mind that humans are fallible and make mistakes. Changes need to be made to recognize that people can learn both from their successes and their failures. The process of saying "I'm sorry" requires a change in professional cultures, which will take years to achieve. Spending precious health care dollars on creating systems to put into place safeguards and accountability mechanisms can be difficult to justify, although Mr. Thomas stated that all available reports suggest there are savings to be found within the health care system that could pay for the reforms recommended in his report. However, the precise cost/benefit ratio is difficult to analyze.

As well, the report was critical of the lack of formal recognition of the unique, expanded and critical role nurses now play within the health care system. The profession has evolved and the scientific, research, managerial and ethical components of nursing education have been expanded and strengthened. Nurses now assume duties once assigned to physicians. The knowledge and education gap between the physician and the nurse has shrunk over the past few decades. The most important fact is that nurses still have the most contact with their patients. They are with them around the clock.

Yet there is still a huge nursing shortage which no one seems to be able to resolve. Retention and recruitment seem to be catchwords of the day. Delegations travel to foreign countries to recruit, but retention is the key. Bringing new foreign nurses is a good thing, but it is costly and time-consuming, and comes with its own set of problems. Keeping the nurses we have seems to be a more practical solution, as is increasing the numbers of new grads the university programs turn out.

Nurses take on a huge amount of responsibility and are accountable for their professional conduct, but they still have very little power to affect change within the system. There is still reluctance within the health care

system to accept nurses as professional equals with an important contri-
bution to make to the care of their patients.

In his opening paragraph under "Final Thoughts," Mr. Thomas wrote:

> We began this report by calling attention to the complex and
> dynamic nature of the health care system. If the health care
> system once sailed along relatively calm waters, it now seems
> to face conditions of permanent 'white water' involving
> constant review and change. During recent decades, there
> have been few, if any, opportunities in the health system
> for individuals and institutions to fully absorb one wave
> of change before another wave crashes down upon them.
>
> Consideration of this report and implementation of its
> recommendations will absorb further time and energies of
> the dedicated professionals and others who work within the
> Manitoba heath care system.

In the end, despite the best intentions of the people involved, there
are limits to the scope and speed of changes that the health care system
can successfully achieve during any given time.

Several years later, Mr. Thomas outlined several key initiatives since
the committee's report. They included the creation of the Western Canada
Children's Heart Network (WCCHN), which serves children with cardiac
problems and their families in four provinces: Manitoba, Saskatchewan,
Alberta, and British Columbia. Other initiatives included, improved
informed consent, on-line physician profiles, critical incident reporting
and The Apology Act.

In February 2002, Manitoba Health and Healthy Living began to
develop provincial policies for the key areas of the recommendations.
Working groups were set up with representatives from the Health Sciences
Centre, all regional health authorities, the College of Physicians and
Surgeons of Manitoba, the Office of the Chief Medical Examiner, and
Manitoba Health and Healthy Living. Other organizations referenced
were CancerCare Manitoba, The Addictions Foundation of Manitoba and
the Selkirk Mental Health Centre. In the summary of the 2008 report,
Thomas notes the health authorities have addressed and incorporated the

policies of the Review and Recommendation committee into their day-to-day operations as required. The final report included a "Score Card," which listed fifty-three completed recommendations.

PROBABLY THE MOST SIGNIFICANT of Justice Sinclair's recommendations was his ruling that all pediatric heart surgeries in Western Canada be done in one or two centres. The WCCHN was officially established in 2001. The motto of the network is *Four Provinces, Five children's hospitals and One heartbeat.*

Five centres are now involved in the care of children with cardiac problems: The Health Sciences Centre (Children's) in Winnipeg, The Stollery Children's Hospital in Edmonton, Alberta Children's Hospital in Calgary, Jim Pattison Children's Centre in Saskatoon, and the BC Children's Hospital in Vancouver.

Between them, the hospitals provide services in pediatric cardiac surgery, pediatric cardiac transplant surgery, pediatric electrophysiological services (the study of electrical activity within the heart), pediatric catheterization, cardiac MRIs, and follow-up care for cardiology services.

Before 2001, four of the five centres across the West (including Winnipeg) had pediatric cardiac surgery programs. Now there are only two.

The new network provides optimal pediatric cardiac care in all centres for all children in the four western provinces. Their database houses important data on patients cared for within the network, including diagnoses, treatments, outcomes and more. The network is based around collaboration and share clinical results, share patient and family resources, provide education, and work together on complex cases. It is one of the largest child cardiac databases in North America.

In Winnipeg, pediatric cardiac services are provided both on an outpatient basis and in hospital at HSC. The team provides care to infants, children, and adolescents with genetic cardiac conditions, cardiac complications and cardiac defects that require medical management.

Today, the Children's Heart Centre is run by wonderful competent staff. Children get excellent care, and if necessary are transferred through the WCCHN to the larger centres west of Manitoba for surgery.

AS I WAS WRITING THIS, I was put in touch with Donald Lepp, some-one who knew intimately how the WCCHN worked. His book, *Heart Broken: Our Family's Story of Surviving Medical Tragedy* chronicled his family's experiences of waiting for a heart transplant for their newborn son, Russell, in 2008. He has kindly allowed me to share some of his perspectives as a parent of a desperately ill child in Manitoba's current pediatric care environment. His connections with the Children's Heart Centre here in Winnipeg provided some valuable insight into what par-ents go through these days. His son, born in August 2008, had a rare condition called Non-Compaction, a form of cardiomyopathy and needed a new heart. This was surgery that could not be done in Winnipeg. He was transferred to the Stollery Centre in Edmonton where he received expert care until a heart was found.

Tiny two-month-old Izayah from Seattle, a victim of homicide, was the donor. On December 30, 2008, at 1:45 p.m., he was removed from life support and his heart was flown to Edmonton. Coincidentally, Izayah was born on October 2, the same day Russell went to the Emergency Room with heart problems. As Donald puts it in his book, "A tragedy for one family was a triumph for another."

Donald and his wife stayed with Russell at Stollery until it was safe to take him back to Winnipeg, where he spent time in the PICU at Winnipeg's Children's Hospital before he was discharged home.

Donald describes his family's experiences in Edmonton in great detail. The other twist to the story is that his wife Susan also had a form of con-genital cardiomyopathy and required urgent heart surgery shortly after Russell's. Although Donald doesn't give a "review" of the care his son and the family received during their time in Edmonton, his descriptions of the events they experienced and the staff they encountered during this highly difficult and stressful time make it clear that this was certainly the place to be for a problem as serious and complex as Russell's.

Although the process was understandably an emotional rollercoast-er, Donald says the support from the cardiac teams in Winnipeg and Edmonton were comforting and thorough. Things went wrong from time to time but as parents, they were always dealt with in a timely, professional, and knowledgeable manner. This was the "right" place and time to go through this process rather than 1994, which had clearly been the "wrong" place and time.

His son's health care issues turned Lepp into a speaker, writer, and vocal advocate for patient and family care. He had even sat on the board of directors of the WRHA for several years. He gives great credit to Murray Sinclair's inquest and report on the 1994 deaths for the changes in cardiac care. In an unpublished essay, he noted "We were one of the lucky ones—we came later. Our cardiac journey would take place at a much different place and time."

Lepp saw the former judge and senator at the Winnipeg airport and felt he had to introduce himself:

> I felt a little urgency and I got right to the reason for the introduction. "I just wanted to say thanks. I am one of the cardiac families seen at the Variety Heart Centre." That comment caught Sinclair's attention and the reason for the introduction now became apparent. He started to speak—nothing of consequence but an acknowledge-ment of work that he had taken on many years before. Something that should have been a distant memory but had such meaningful impact that will likely never be for-gotten. Especially for the families with congenital heart disease in Manitoba.

Lepp writes:

> The journey that my son took was a direct result of this unassuming man I met by chance on the Winnipeg air-port. Events that were set in motion nearly 25 years earlier. Events that echoed many years afterward. This assertion was confirmed by the man at the airport who shared with me how he still kept in contact with some of the families who were impacted by the tragic events that took place in the early '90s.

The author has nothing but praise for the Sinclair inquest's recommendations, "but I think far too much emphasis and credit has been given to bureaucratic nuance that looked good on paper but translated into very little to do with the pediatric cardiac program itself." In his essay, Lepp noted there have been institutional changes like critical incident legislation, the set up of local health involvement groups, and the Institute for Patient Safety that may someday make Manitoba a leader in patient safety. But he says the real change came from determined individuals like those at the Variety Children's Heart Centre.

After pediatric cardiac surgery was shut down, a toxic work environment remained that would have been beyond the ability of most to cope. In the "dark time" from 1994 to 2000, children still had heart problems. Lepp recounts the story of one family that moved to Edmonton to be closer to a hospital that could provide better care. Some families took their child home, convinced the diagnosis was terminal. Other families went to Toronto or the Mayo Clinic.

The few staff that were left at the end of 1994 were completely overwhelmed. But Lepp writes that centre's staff understood that pediatric cardiac surgery was never coming back to the HSC. Instead of lamenting that fact, they embraced it. They found creative ways to reroute sick children to other centres. The specter of the cardiac deaths was so politically charged, government routinely approved travel plans for kids and their families. The Western Canadian Children's Heart Network was taking shape in the late 1990s, even before the inquest asked for it.

By the time Russell's heart problems were diagnosed, Lepp wrote,

> We felt completely embraced by how they were open with us—they seemed to have their act together. Of course, we had things go wrong, but even when mistakes happened, it seemed to strengthen the relationship with our team because we got information—and we were being coached and supported and we felt like part of the team. Nothing remotely close to the complete disrespect shown to families as described in the judicial inquest. Why such a different experience?

OVER THE YEARS, people have often asked me if something like what happened in 1994 could happen again. Because I was no longer practicing as a nurse within the health care system, I found that question to be difficult if not impossible to answer. I asked Donald Lepp and Paul Thomas what their thoughts were. Both said it was an important question. Both gave me some of their insights into the health care system, past and present. And both said the answer was Yes and No.

Could this happen within Manitoba's Pediatric Cardiology Department now? The answer was an emphatic NO. The department as it stands now is part of the WCCHN and so they operate within that network. Any surgical issues are dealt with in the programs set up where the children would be sent out for surgery. All diagnostics and lab data are shared within the network to make sure that all involved know who the patient is and what the problem is. Decisions are made about treatment and surgery by a team of specialists, not in isolation. The children of Manitoba with heart problems now get excellent state-of-the-art care.

In response to tragedies like the 1994 baby deaths, and the resulting inquest, governments and regulatory bodies for health professions have placed more emphasis on patient safety. The culture is changing from a "blaming" to a "learning" response to human error. Other mechanisms include critical incident legislation, whereby the ways incidents are investigated are completely different now. The Apology Act, which received royal assent in 2007, "allows a person to make an apology about a matter without the apology constituting an admission of legal liability." The Public Interest Disclosure (Whistle Blower Protection) Act (PIDA) received royal assent in 2008. Its purpose is to "facilitate the disclosure and investigation of significant and serious matters in or related to the public bodies, and protects employees who make disclosures from reprisal."

These legislative acts encourage health care professionals to acknowledge mistakes without the fear of reprisal and legal liability. In addition, there are far more robust human resource practices in place and more due diligence in the hiring process than in 1994. None of these reforms are perfect but they represent improvement.

One of the biggest changes after the inquest was the advent of patient-and family-centred care (PFCC). That is the practice of allowing families to remain with their loved ones and to be part of the decision-making process. During COVID, keeping families separated and restricting information all came back, unfortunately. Donald Lepp worries that some of the old barriers have been resurrected and that it will be difficult to go back to how things were pre-COVID.

Unfortunately, there can never be a completely safe health care system because there are many factors involved, including human error. But with the advent of some of the changes to the system, I hope that the chances of a tragedy of the magnitude like the one I experienced in 1994 will never happen again. Of late, however, government cutbacks, under-staffing, excessive overtime, fatigue and burnout have created heightened risks for situations where mistakes can occur.

CHAPTER 25

IN CELEBRATION OF NURSES

It is 2023 and COVID-19 has been with us for more than three years with no signs of letting up. We see variant after variant, one on the heels of the other. Vaccines save lives, of course, but people are still getting sick. There's an old saying that there is no such thing as a cure for the common cold. It has been a problem forever, and we produce a vaccine to fight it every year. And every year, we take a chance that we are going to get it right and aim it at the right virus or variant.

COVID-19 overtaxed a health care system that was already at the breaking point. Where I live, health care cuts designed to cut costs were chipping away at an already fragile system. Mandatory overtime, resulting in nurses working sixteen to twenty-hour shifts, is common now. Nurses work without breaks. They are called in on their days off, vacation time is cancelled. Nurses, doctors and other health care professionals are at the breaking point. Burnout is becoming common, nurses are leaving, not because they want to but because they have to. They can't carry this load forever. Doctors and nurses make regular pleas to the government for help, all of which seem to fall on deaf ears.

Recently, I saw a woman interviewed about her career change. She had been a critical care nurse for years but couldn't take it any longer and became a long-distance trucker. She drives her semi all over Canada and the United States and is much happier. She hates that fact that she had to leave the profession she loves, but her mental and physical health were deteriorating to the breaking point.

Hospitals are spending millions on agency nurses to cover shifts. These nurses are paid more and have total control over when they work. Many nurses from the hospital system are leaving their jobs for agency jobs where they can pick and choose their hours. Some nurses work both systems: on staff at a hospital part-time and an agency as well. They can continue to get some of their benefits from the hospital and still get to control their work-life balance by working for an agency too. I can't blame them.

This is what those of us who are either working in the system or have in the past wonder: Why are the people making the decisions accountants or "bean counters," who are for the most part linear thinkers. They are always focused on the bottom line. They think about today or this month or this year, but they don't seem to realize that there are long-term ramifications resulting from the cuts they make. They miss the big picture. They aren't listening to the frontline workers, the people who actually know what is going on. The doctors and nurses who walk into an emergency room or ICU full of critically ill people are the ones who should be consulted about what is going to bring about meaningful change.

Nurses had to fight for proper PPE (personal protection equipment) at the onset of the pandemic. There were stories of staff reusing masks and wearing garbage bags for protection. Nurses got sick. One study from the Canadian Institute of Health in early 2021 showed 65,920 health care workers were infected with COVID-19, almost ten percent of the infections in Canada. But those that could kept showing up for work, out of care and concern for the sickest people who were hospitalized. Despite all this data, and efforts by their unions, health care workers were still put into unacceptable positions of risk to themselves, their families and their communities.

Politicians talk about these "health care heroes" and how much we appreciate them. However, when it comes down to it, no substantive assistance, such as more staff, better hours, better PPE, or better pay seem forthcoming. Nurses who have left the profession for a period of time for various reasons such as illness, injury, or childcare issues and who wanted to come back to help out during the pandemic had to be reinstated by our regulatory body, the College of Registered Nurses of Manitoba. The cost of renewing their nursing license was prohibitive to many. Recertification courses are necessary and expensive. Many gave up or worked for a much lower wage at the vaccination and testing sites. Foreign-trained nurses have a difficult time registering through the College in our province. While most are well trained, there are professional standards that must be met. The public needs to be protected. Recruitment is important. Retention is the key. Find a way to keep the nurses we have.

In 2023, a delegation including our health minister and nursing managers travelled to the Philippines to recruit nurses for our province. News reports indicated they were successful. Several years ago, places in the Bachelor of Nurses Program at the University of Manitoba were cut from 250 to 150. This year it was announced that thirty spaces were to be reinstated. This appears to be a visible effort to mitigate the damage inflicted by the previous cuts.

At the end of the day, there continues to be a desperate need for more staff. Budget cuts over the past few years have eroded the health care system and the quality of patient care everywhere. Many nurses believe that if decision makers had heeded nurses' warnings prior to the pandemic, it is possible that many more lives could have been saved.

As a nurse who has worked in critical care, I know how difficult it can be to work in an ICU on a "normal" day. I can only imagine the hell these people must have gone through every single day.

I have to wonder why people who have, for the most part, never set foot in an ICU feel they should be making decisions which directly impact the patients and their caregivers. It seems that many decisions are based on political or financial reasons, not medical or scientific information. Because health care is a provincial matter, each province controls their purse strings. The federal government allocates money to each province for health care and the provinces always ask for more.

It has been said nurses along with other health care professionals have kept the system from collapsing under the weight of the influx of critically ill COVID patients. At the beginning of each COVID wave, health care workers, usually ICU or ER doctors, warned of the impending implosion of the system. Somehow they found the strength to be there for their critically ill patients.

Nurses are frontline workers. They are at the bedside and sometimes they have not left that bedside, not even for a bathroom or meal break. They bathe and turn their patients, give complicated treatments and titrate medications that keep them alive. Many of these meds are delivered by infusion pumps at the bedside. There may be ten or twenty of them running at the same time.

Nurses work with the respiratory therapist to keep their patient's oxygen levels steady and life sustaining. They work with physiotherapists, social workers, and other members of the team. When those health care workers are unavailable, the nurses fill in for them and perform their duties as well as their own.

All these health care workers are very important, but they come and go from the bedside. Nurses are the constant presence. They are there throughout their shift. If they do get a break, another nurse steps in to relieve them. Ideally, the patient-nurse ratio is one to one in the ICU. In that scenario, each patient has their own nurse. The sickest ones often need more than one nurse because their needs are so complex. Those ratios became nearly impossible to maintain because of the numbers of critically ill patients being admitted.

Nurses are the communicators, speaking with doctors and other health care workers, alerting them to critical changes in their patient's condition based on their observations. These observations are done on a minute by minute, second by second basis and the treatment the patient receives changes as the patient either recovers or deteriorates.

Nurses are teachers, educating patients, family, and the general public on health-related issues. They are often the professional people turn to for advice in such matters.

Families trust the nurse because they know that for the most part it is the nurse who knows what is really going on and it is the nurse who will communicate this with them in an honest and compassionate way. They are there, at the bedside, all day and all night. As the numbers climbed and the hospitals filled up with desperately ill people, it was the nurses who were at the forefront. The COVID patients kept coming in. More and more, and sicker and sicker as the weeks went by.

Are there beds for all these people? Yes, physically there are actual beds sitting there empty, because there is no nurse. When a hospital says there are no more beds available, what they are really saying is that there are no more nurses available. Put a patient in that bed and there would be no one to care for them.

Finally, nurses are the glue that holds all the other professions involved with the care of a patient together. Doctors count on the bedside nurse to let them know what is going on. Often they make the doctor look good. Nearly every nurse I know has a story about how they saved a doctor's ass at some point in their career. Maybe by questioning a medication choice or dosage, or a treatment that might not be appropriate at the time. Often these physicians are exhausted too, and errors are made. Some of the best doctors I have worked with were former nurses or started off getting a nursing degree but switched to medicine at some point before graduating.

COVID HAS SHOWN US ALL how important nursing really is. Nurses are evolving to meet the pressure: we work with it, we work through it, we meet the needs of these patients to the best of our ability, and if the time comes when we can do no more, we are there, quietly holding their hand as they leave this world. I think the saddest thing about the pandemic is the fact that so many people had to die alone, without their loved ones nearby. As a nurse, I know this would be heartbreaking to witness. If it was my family member, I know I would carry that extra piece of grief forever.

Nurses are knowledge, expertise, dedication, compassion all rolled up into one (often exhausted) body. Nursing isn't about fluffing pillows and wiping fevered brows, it is literally about making the difference between life and death.

CHAPTER 26

ALMOST THE END

It is now 2023. I started writing this in 2021. It had been years since I had really sat down and thought about it all, though it has always there, in the back of my mind. People, friends, family, neighbours asked me about it over the years.

I retired from my job at the Medical Examiner's Office in 2010 when I was in my early sixties and found that I missed the work and the people. I was happy to go back to help out and I stayed on part-time for a few more years. I still miss the work, but retirement has had its benefits, although the COVID-19 pandemic has made it somewhat difficult in terms of getting out and about with my friends and family these past three years.

I took up some hobbies… painting (enjoyable, but I am not very talented), sourdough bread making (delicious but fattening), knitting (maybe a bit of a disaster), and now writing (time will tell). All these pursuits, as well as some physical activities (walking and aquafit classes) that were curtailed due to the pandemic and a brutally cold and snowy and icy winter, made the weeks fly by. Friends drop in, we "do lunch," go shopping and life is good. The latest activity is learning how to play Mahjong, which has been an interesting and fun experience.

I embarked on this project last summer after hearing for the umpteenth time that I should write a book. I talked to Colleen about it, and she was very encouraging. I got in touch with some people in the business who gave me some advice regarding publishing and other issues. I had no idea how it all worked and as I go along, I am learning so much. I found that I enjoyed writing and with some help from Steve Donahue, my book coach, I have found this process to be very interesting and rewarding. It was both cathartic and difficult.

It has certainly brought back many memories, and some are very painful. When I feel that it is getting to me again, I stop and take a break for a couple of days. That seems to help, and I can go back to it with a clear head.

My main concern as I write about these twelve kids is their families and how this book might open old wounds. I want to honour these children by telling their stories. As far as I know, no one has written a book about what happened. I felt that since I was one of the few people who was involved with all but one case, I could try to do them justice. Looking back on it now, from the distance of time, proves to me that the program should have been halted and the surgeon's skills evaluated long before December 1994.

I read somewhere that in several surveys of the most trusted professions, nurses ALWAYS come out in the number one spot. Doctors are usually a few professions down the list. That doesn't mean that doctors can't be trusted. The majority of them are out there working hard every day to meet the needs of their patients. We all worked within a system and when it works, as it usually does, people get great care. That was my experience over the many years I worked at Children's and HSC. I think the majority, if not all my nursing colleagues, would agree. That is where I advised people to go when they needed expert care.

What happened in 1994 was an anomaly. A gathering storm of circumstances, the loss of an experienced surgeon and senior cardiologists, the program run by two relatively junior people, likely with big ambitions and the absence of mentorship and advice from senior people around the Centre. On top of that, warning signals were either misinterpreted or ignored.

Nurses are the frontline workers. They go in every day, and they save lives every day. They don't get a pat on the back very often, and they don't expect it. They just want to do their job as best they can, for their patients.

I hope I learned something about accountability and compassion during the good, the bad and the ugly times I worked as a nurse. It is a profession that demands a lot from those of us who do it. Some nurses say it's a calling. I never felt that way. To me it was an interesting and fulfilling profession. On a good day, I loved it. On a bad day, I found it challenging and frustrating. On the ugly days in 1994, I often wondered why I had ever chosen this profession.

It takes its toll, like any other profession where one works with people in crisis. These events affected me deeply. More so than I realized at the time. Mostly because so much of it was preventable.

Writing about it was hard but I have come to terms with my role in it and that of the other members of the team, who tried to draw attention to the problems we faced. I doubt that any of us will forget or completely get over what happened.

I can only hope that I told my story well and that anyone reading this will gain a further understanding of what nurses do, what we aspire to and how we feel about our patients, especially the tiny and vulnerable children who are unlucky enough to need our services. They deserve the best care possible.

GARY CARIBOU
- Six months, twenty days old
- The evidence suggests that this death was possibly preventable.

JESSICA ULIMAUMI
- Seven months, nine days old
- The evidence suggests that this death was preventable.

VINAY GOYAL
- Four years, one month, sixteen days old
- The evidence suggests that this death was preventable.

DANIEL TERZISKI
- Thirty-three days old
- The evidence suggests that had Daniel been referred out of province for his surgery, the chance of preventing this death would have been increased.

ALYSSA STILL
- Five months, twenty-two days old
- The evidence suggests that this death might have been preventable.

SHALYNN PILLER
- Fourteen days old
- The evidence suggests that it was not possible to determine whether her death was preventable.

ARIC BAUMANN
- Eight months, fourteen days old
- The evidence suggests that this was not a preventable death.

MARIETESS TENA CAPILI
- Two years, nine months old
- The evidence suggests that this was a preventable death.

ERICA BICHEL
· Five days old
· The evidence suggests that although she would have had a better chance of survival in the hands of a more experienced surgeon and surgical team, this death was likely not preventable.

ASHTON FEAKES
· One year, three months and twenty-seven days old
· The evidence suggests that this death was preventable.

JESSE MAGUIRE
· Two days old
· The evidence suggests that this was a preventable death.

ERIN PETKAU
· Three days old
· The evidence suggests that this death was possibly preventable.

THANK YOU

Colleen Suche and Bill Gange, lawyers for the nurses. They got it. They got us. They empowered us. We spoke the truth and we were believed.

To my parents, Ernie and Ethel Jackson, both schoolteachers who instilled in me the love of books and knowledge. Long gone now, but I know you would be proud.

Ron Youngson AKA the LSS ... Long Suffering Spouse. He supported me during the lengthy court process back then. Even though we aren't together now, he has remained one of my best friends and is enthusiastically supportive of this endeavor.

My son, Josh Youngson. In early 1994 when these events took place, he was only nine years old. I tried not to let him know what was going on at the time. He was living his childhood, happy and worry free (I hope!). He's now a wonderful young man who has been so positive and supportive.

My daughter-in-law Vanessa. She had enthusiastically encouraged and supported me as well.

The late Diana Davidson Dick who in 1994, was the Director of the Manitoba Association of Registered Nurses (now known as The College of Registered Nurses of Manitoba). She understood the need for nurses to have separate standing, good legal advice, and a voice at a time when we might well have been silenced or worse, scapegoated.

Steve Donahue, at www.storyglu.com, my book coach from the start. We worked together for almost two years. He was always kind, encouraging, and enthusiastic, and guided me skillfully through a process that I often did not understand. He taught me a lot about writing and publishing, and I could not have done this without his assistance. On a couple of occasions when it all got to me, he would assure me that all this wasn't my fault.

Graham Wilcox, another editor who helped me out toward the end… tidying up.

Ingeborg Boyens, my main editor, whom I might have driven crazy from time to time… fixing and fiddling even when she told me not to. I still think the Bee Gees' song was a good idea.

Catharina de Bakker, another editor who went through this manuscript word by word, sentence by sentence, paragraph by paragraph. Her attention to detail impressed me. Even when I thought I had it all covered there were still improvements to be made.

Dr. Kim Duncan, Pediatric Cardiac Surgeon. Thank you for sharing your expertise and time with me. I enjoyed and appreciated our conversations about all this. I hope I did it well.

To our employer's lawyers, I will always be grateful not to have had you representing the nurses. Whatever your reasons were, you did us a favour.

My sisters Nancy Brown and Kathy Stasiuk and my brother Gerry Westlake. Always there for me, even though they often didn't know what the heck I was talking about! They gave me their unconditional support. I love you guys!

Nursing friends and classmates: They understood the hierarchy and issues that nurses faced in those days. Many came to court and sat quietly in the gallery to support me. I could look over at them from time to time and I took great comfort from their presence. Lynn, Margaret, Barbara, thanks for your encouragement and for letting me talk (likely ad nauseam) about "The Book". To the other nurses in my life, classmates, co-workers over the years, thanks for making going to work so enjoyable and rewarding for most of my career.

To the "Broken Hearts Club": Irene Hinam, Carol Dupuis, Donna Feser, Deb Armitage and Joan Borton (both now deceased), we stood together and tried to make a change. None of us will forget the events of 1994. Elaine Bennett, a psych nurse, who we met professionally as a critical incident supporter back then. You stood by us and helped us maintain some sanity during a very difficult time. You're now our friend. Thanks!

Nursing colleagues everywhere, who were so supportive to us. For a few years after this all happened, we gave presentations at nursing meetings and conferences. We were always warmly received and often approached afterwards by nurses with similar stories to tell. They thanked us for our courage and dedication to our patients. We received standing ovations every time.

Neighbors and friends who listened and probably heard more about what happens in an OR than they wanted to.

MARN, now known as College of Registered Nurses of Manitoba. On the advice of Diana, you found and hired Colleen and Bill who became like family. We were always welcome at their offices, and they made themselves available to us whenever we needed them. We appreciated the support of the staff and executive at MARN at the time.

I am so grateful to Paul Thomas who assisted me in some of the follow up, after the release of Judge Sinclair's report and the subsequent Thomas Report (Report of the Review and Implementation Committee for the Report of the Manitoba Pediatric Cardiac Surgery Inquest).

Thanks to Donald Lepp who is such an advocate for patient and family-based care. Thank you for sharing your story with me and for being so generous with your information and time. Your book *Heart Broken: Our Family's Story of Surviving Medical Tragedy* is a must-read for anyone dealing with a child with a catastrophic illness.

Thanks to my publisher, Great Plains Press for taking a chance on me. Thanks to Mel Marginet and Keith Cadieux for all their efforts to get this book "out there".

Finally thank you to my readers. People have asked me about these events over the years and upon hearing some of the details often inquire as to why I haven't written a book. Frankly, I have often wondered why no one did before now. Having said that, I decided that it was time.

SUMMARY OF THE INQUIRY FINDINGS

In addition to reporting on the children's unique cases, Judge Sinclair also asked questions that explored themes that the cases had in common:

WERE THE PARENTS GIVEN ENOUGH INFORMATION TO PROVIDE AN INFORMED CONSENT?

In all twelve cases, the judge found that the parents were not given enough information to provide an informed consent. They were not told that Dr. Odim had never performed some of the operations on his own. They were not told about the slowdown in the spring and the Wiseman Committee meetings, and they were often discouraged from having their child sent out of the province to a bigger centre and a more experienced surgeon.

WAS THE CHILD HEALTHY ENOUGH FOR SURGERY AT THAT TIME?

Timing is important. In the cases of Gary, Jessica, Daniel, Alyssa and Ashton, the child was either not in optimal condition for surgery due to an infection, or in Ashton's case, delayed over the summer when the slowdown occurred. He should likely have been sent out at that point but was forced to wait until the full program resumed.

WAS THE SKILL AND DEXTERITY OF THE SURGEON SUFFICIENT TO SUCCESSFULLY PERFORM THE PROCEDURE?

Three of the first three VSD repairs died (Gary, Jessica and Vinay). One expert witness stated that those deaths should have been enough to cause concern and perhaps a review of the program to date. Based on those results, Daniel and Erica (Norwood operations) should have been sent out for surgery. Alyssa's coronary sinus was inadvertently sewn over. Marietess, Jesse, and Erin were all deemed possibly preventable due to Dr. Odim's actions. Shalynn and Ashton should have been sent out. Only Aric, who had a serious, inoperable and unidentified heart defect could not have survived. His was the only death that had been acceptably explained.

In Marietess's case, expert witness Dr. Christian Soder, an anesthetist from Halifax, said it so well: "I would have locked the door. There is no way I would have accepted a medical explanation for what I was seeing." In his comments after reviewing the deaths of several of the other children he wrote: "**The skill and dexterity of the surgeon performing these operations were insufficient for the challenge of successfully repairing infant hearts with complex malformations. Surgical factors were the prime determinants of fatal outcome in nine of the twelve deaths.**" [boldface in original]

There were many findings having to do with how the hospital ran the Pediatric Cardiac Surgery Program prior to and during 1994. Some are listed, verbatim, below. My own summaries are provided in italics. The entire report can be accessed publicly at pediatriccardiacinquest.mb.ca.

THE LOSS AND RECRUITMENT OF THE PROGRAM STAFF BEFORE 1994

FINDING:

· The evidence suggests that the loss of and failure to replace professional medical staff from the Variety Children's Heart Centre in 1992 and 1993 represented a serious erosion in the ability of the Pediatric Cardiac Surgery Program to continue to provide the level of services that it had previously provided.

· The evidence suggests that the impact on the program of the loss of the medical staff in and before 1993 was not appreciated by the heads of the responsible departments.

· The evidence suggests the HSC's recruitment of a pediatric cardiac surgeon in 1993 to replace Dr. Kim Duncan was flawed.

· The evidence suggests that the process of replacing Dr. George Collins as head of the Variety Children's Heart Centre following his retirement in 1993 was flawed.

RECOMMENDATION:
It is recommended that the HSC establish a medical staff recruitment process for senior or specialized positions within the hospital that has as its main priority the creation of a mechanism that results in the best possible candidate being hired or appointed.

THE COMPENSATION PAID TO PEDIATRIC CARDIAC SURGEONS

FINDING:

· The manner in which cardiac surgeons are financially compensated in Manitoba is not satisfactory.

RECOMMENDATION:

It is recommended that the Manitoba government and the Manitoba Medical Association adjust the Manitoba doctors' fee schedule to allow for the payment of compensation to pediatric cardiac surgeons that does not stand in the way of the effective recruiting of, and maintenance of, pediatric cardiac surgeons in Manitoba.

PROBLEMS WITHIN THE PEDIATRIC CARDIAC SURGERY PROGRAM

FINDING:

- The evidence establishes that the responsibility for the Pediatric Cardiac Surgery Program at the HSC was jointly held by the head of the Department of Surgery and the Department of Pediatrics.

- The evidence establishes that the lines of authority and responsibility for the Pediatric Cardiac Surgery Program were unclear and confusing to hospital staff during 1994.

RECOMMENDATION:

It is recommended that if a Pediatric Cardiac Surgery Program is re-established at the HSC, it have clear written lines of authority and responsibility. Efforts must be made to ensure that program members understand these lines of authority. This is of particular importance in a multidisciplinary program.

THE RESPONSIBILITY OF DR. JONAH ODIM AND DR. NIELS GIDDINS FOR THE EVENTS OF 1994

FINDING:

- The evidence suggests that neither Dr. Odim nor Dr. Giddins carried out their responsibilities to monitor and respond suitably to the poor surgical results in the program.

RECOMMENDATION:

No recommendations were made for this finding.

MISUSING THE CONCEPT OF A "LEARNING CURVE"

FINDING:

· The evidence suggests that the acceptance of a learning curve muted the degree of concern that Drs. Odim, Giddins and Wiseman should have had when surgical nurses and anesthetists voiced concerns about surgical results.

Judge Sinclair wrote further that the concept of a learning curve can be abused. In other words, there should be no room for the consideration of a learning curve if the safety or wellbeing of a patient is at risk or when analyzing the results of an operation. In the early part of this surgeon's experience, it was deemed part of the learning process and this, Judge Sinclair found, was not an appropriate use of the concept. Further, he stated that morbidity and mortality rates are known to be higher during the early days of the development of a program. They are certainly found to be higher if the program does not have a carefully planned and initiated start up. Drs. Blanchard, Bishop, Odim and Giddins all bear responsibility in that they should have individually and collectively ensured that the program was restarted on a carefully phased basis.

ADMINISTRATIVE ISSUES

FINDING:

· The evidence suggests that Drs. Blanchard and Bishop, the department heads responsible for the program, did not address the underlying issues that led to the departure of Drs. Collins and Duncan. Instead, the program was placed in the hands of a relatively inexperienced cardiologist and an even more junior surgeon who had just completed his training.

· The evidence suggests that Drs. Blanchard and Bishop failed to recognize that, in light of the significant changes in personnel at the Variety Children's Heart Centre, the lack of experience of the new leadership of the Pediatric Cardiac Surgery Program, and the fact that the cardiologists who had left the program in the previous year and a half had not yet been replaced, the program would require close supervision and monitoring in early 1994. *I think this meant that no one was watching or monitoring the new surgeon.*

- The evidence suggests that Drs. Blanchard and Bishop furthermore did not prepare for or have in place a proper orientation for either a new surgeon or a new director of the VCHC. Giddins was assigned interim responsibility for the position vacated by Collins, but there is no evidence that he was prepared for the duties he was assigned.

- The evidence suggests that Drs. Blanchard and Bishop, along with Giddins, also did not ensure that there was either formal or informal monitoring of Dr. Odim upon his arrival at the HSC. In the case of a young surgeon in his first appointment following his residency, more careful consideration ought to have been given to the fact that he was facing an entirely different experience from what he had faced as a surgical resident.

- The evidence suggests that Drs. Bishop, Blanchard, along with Giddins, also did not ensure that anyone was assigned responsibility or took responsibility for building and mentoring the Pediatric Cardiac Surgery team as a whole in the early part of 1994. Without this leadership, the problems that arose in the early operations rapidly led to unre-solved—and in the end, unresolvable—conflicts. *Judge Sinclair stated further that the program was plagued with very serious problems and the OR and ICUs were not properly prepared for Dr. Odim's particular approach to surgery and post-operative care.*

- The evidence suggests that Drs. Bishop, Blanchard, Giddins and Odim did not give sufficient consideration to Dr. Odim's lack of experience and to the level of team experience.

- The evidence suggests that the lack of supervision and the lack of a phased start-up plan meant that the Pediatric Cardiac Surgery Program was marked by poor case selection in 1994 and that the program undertook cases that were beyond the skill and experience of the surgeon and the team.

- The evidence suggests that the cardiologist and the surgeon did not take appropriate steps to establish and maintain open and ongoing lines of communication with other related medical services, such as nursing and anesthesia.

Additionally, the Judge commented that the surgeon must have erroneously assumed that everyone knew what he was talking about and there was a lack of sufficient consultation and briefing before the team undertook specific complicated procedures. For example, it seemed clear that the NICU team was not briefed or adequately prepared to receive Dr. Odim's patients undergoing Norwood procedures.

RECOMMENDATION:

It is recommended that the HSC develop protocols for providing orientation and support to all new staff and staff moving into new positions. This should be done even when the appointment is to an acting position.

It is recommended that any re-established Pediatric Cardiac Surgery Program involve all units that would be affected by the program in the development of the appropriate protocols. Such protocols should include a requirement that the entire team, including those individuals responsible for post-operative care, be fully prepared before the program moves to higher-risk cases or new procedures.

INAPPROPRIATE STAFFING LEVELS

FINDING:

- The evidence suggests that Drs. Blanchard and Bishop, the department heads responsible for the program at the relevant time, appeared to have failed to recognize the full implications of only one cardiologist being at the VCHC for most of 1994. Steps should have been taken to limit the number of patients seen, on the basis of Dr. Giddins's workload alone.

- The evidence suggests that the fact that, throughout the existence of this program, there was only one surgeon who was on constant call, also placed a high degree of pressure on the surgeon.

- A shortage in the Department of Pathology also contributed to the fact that autopsy reports were not completed in a timely manner.

- The evidence suggests that an appropriate balance had not been struck between the number of anesthetists providing care to the program and the number of cases in which each anesthetist participated.

RECOMMENDATION:

It is recommended that the restart of the Pediatric Cardiac Surgery Program be initiated only after the relevant department heads jointly review staffing levels and assure themselves that they are appropriate to avoid overwork and fatigue and maintain appropriate skill levels.

More specifically it is recommended that:

- Any restart of the Pediatric Cardiac Surgery Program be initiated only at a time when pediatric cardiology is staffed appropriately.

- If the number of cardiologists is reduced following a restart, the program should reduce the level of service it provides.

- Any new PCSP have provisions for relief for the pediatric cardiac surgeon. This could include protocols for referral of patients out of province or arrangements to bring other surgeons into Manitoba.

- The Department of Surgery of the HSC establish guidelines and protocols for surgeons that help in the decision as to when to operate if fatigued: for example, after being on call. These guidelines and protocols could be similar to those used by anesthetists.

- The Department of Pathology be properly staffed so as to be able to comply with reasonable guidelines for the completion of autopsies and autopsy reports as set out later in this chapter.

- The Department of Anesthesia ensure that the program has an appropriate number of anesthetists. This number would have to take into account the need for anesthetists to be involved in a sufficient number of cases to enable them to obtain a requisite level of experience, as well as ensuring that they are able to provide appropriate coverage for all cases.

TREATMENT OF THE NURSES

FINDING:

· The evidence suggests that because nursing occupied a subservient position within the HSC structure, issues raised by nurses were not always treated appropriately. Nurses voiced legitimate concerns throughout 1994. They were not treated as full and equal members of the surgical program.

The concerns of the OR nurses, including myself, were dismissed as stemming from an inability to deal emotionally with the deaths of some of the patients. Our concerns with medical issues were rejected because of the view that we did not have the proper training or experience to hold or express them. In addition, while the doctors had a representative on the HSC board, nurses did not.

Because of our traditional role, the legitimacy of our concerns were not treated with respect or recognized in a timely manner and patient care was compromised.

· The evidence suggests that nurses were not allowed to play a role in planning the February 1994 restart of the Pediatric Cardiac Surgery program, even though they formed an essential element of that program.

The concerns of the PICU and NICU nurses over the types of procedures that were to be carried out in the units, for example removing a child from ECMO and closing chests, were not addressed in a timely manner. This resulted in the untimely death of at least one child.

The hospital reorganization of 1994 devalued nurses since it appeared to be driven by a concern to cut costs primarily by reducing staff, the bulk of which was nursing. Throughout that year nurses made proper and appropriate use of the existing channels to voice their concerns. For various reasons, some institutional and some personal, their concerns were not attended to.

They were directed to silence themselves. This left nurses frustrated and distraught. Many of us paid a heavy emotional price. By the time the program ended, at least one nurse, was on the verge of taking her concerns outside the hospital at great risk to her position and career.

RECOMMENDATION:
It is necessary to put into place structures that ensure that all staff can make their concerns known without fear of reprisal. It is also important to ensure that the structure of the HSC be adjusted ensure that the position of nursing does not continue to be a subservient one.

It is recommended that the HSC restructure its Nursing Council to allow nurses to select its membership and to give it responsibility for nursing issues within the hospital. The Nursing Council should have representation on the hospital's governing body and be responsible for monitoring, evaluating and making recommendations pertaining to the nursing profession within the hospital and for nursing care. The council should also serve as a vehicle through which nurses could report incidents, issues and concerns without risk of professional reprisal.

It is recommended that the HSC develop a clear policy on how staff is to report concerns about risks for patients. This policy must ensure that there is no risk to the person making the report.

It is recommended that the province of Manitoba consider passing "Whistle Blowing" legislation to protect nurses and other professionals from reprisal stemming from their disclosure of information arising from a legitimately and reasonably held concern over the medical treatment of patients.

ISSUE OF INFORMED CONSENT

FINDING:
- The evidence suggests that the parents of the children involved in these cases were not as fully informed as they were entitled to be when asked to give consent to surgery on their children.

Judge Sinclair also commented that the parents were not fully informed as to the experience of the surgeon, the surgical risk, the slowdown in May and the decision to perform only low-risk procedures thereafter and the decision to resume full service in September 1994.

RECOMMENDATION:
It is recommended that the Department of Health of the Manitoba Government prepare a patient's rights handbook that, among other things, deals with the issue of informed consent. That handbook should clearly set out that a patient and a parent acting on behalf of a minor have a number or rights, including but not limited to:

· The right to be fully informed before giving consent to medical treatment.

· The right to information about a surgeon's experience in performing a particular procedure, as well as the experience of the hospital and/ or surgical team.

· The right to a second opinion.

· The right to an out-of-province referral in certain circumstances, including where the patient or parent chooses to have a procedure performed by a surgeon or institution with more appropriate experience, and where the surgeon or institution in Manitoba lacks the same experience; and

· The right to have an out-of-province surgeon perform the procedure in Manitoba, provided there is a surgeon willing and able to do the procedure here.

It is recommended that the HSC review its policies on consent and communication with families. All information that is germane to a child's care or to decisions that must be made about a child's care should be provided to those from whom consent is being obtained. In particular, the policy on consent must make it clear that the medical staff treating a patient must be forthright and truthful in disclosing all relevant information to the patient or representative before the procedure in question. The fact that a surgeon has not performed a particular surgical procedure on his or her own in an unsupervised setting in the past must be disclosed.

THE EXPERIENCE OF THE SURGEON

While many members of the medical staff feel that a doctor does not have to inform potential patients of his experience, many of the parents felt strongly that they should have been provided with more information about the program and the surgeon's experience. Many hospital staff felt it was enough to say that Dr. Odim was highly trained, one of the best, or that Winnipeg's program was as capable of anywhere else, but that it was inappropriate to tell families that Dr. Odim had never performed certain operations on his own.

Judge Sinclair found this to be concerning. Other witnesses felt that if the families did not ask about previous experience, the doctor was not obligated to reveal this. Judge Sinclair's comment was interesting:

While the obligation to tell the truth is obvious, it seems illogical that some would see the obligation to be truthful as not encompassing an obligation to disclose a relevant fact.

A surgeon's lack of experience is relevant to the question of whether someone would be willing to entrust their life or the life of a loved one to that surgeon.

INFORMATION ABOUT SURGICAL RISK

The risk factors that were explained to the parents for the procedures undertaken by Dr. Odim were not based on the facts of the situations that the children actually faced in Winnipeg.

Risk factors clearly increase with an inexperienced surgeon. That is a scientifically proven fact.

INFORMATION ABOUT THE MAY 17 WITHDRAWAL
OF SERVICES BY THE ANESTHETISTS

All parents whose children were operated on after May 17, 1994, should have been informed about the anesthetists' withdrawal of services. Information about the Williams and Roy Report and the February 1995 suspension of the program should have been available. The parents should have been informed about the report and allowed to read it. They should have been contacted and informed of the suspension of the program before the decision was made public.

FUNDING FOR THE FAMILIES

FINDING:

· The evidence suggests that the parents were hampered throughout the hearings by the burdens of the costs associated with having a legal counsel present throughout.

RECOMMENDATION:

It is recommended that the Government of Manitoba establish a policy for the payment for counsel for families granted standing at inquests, taking into account the following factors:

1. The length of the proceedings
2. The complexity of the issues.
3. Whether or not the costs of family involvement in the proceeding would be prohibitive to the applicant,
4. Whether or not the presiding judge so recommends on the application by the family.

It is recommended that the Government of Manitoba pay the entire legal costs of the families involve in these proceedings.

MONITORING OF ISSUES AND PROBLEMS WITHIN THE HSC

FINDING:

- The evidence suggests that the formal and informal monitoring of issues at the HSC failed to identify the problems with the Pediatric Cardiac Surgery Program in a timely fashion.

- The evidence suggests that Drs. Blanchard and Bishop, the department heads responsible for the program at the relevant time, as well as the cardiologist and the surgeon did not adequately monitor surgical performances and results of the PCS program on either a case-by-case or collective basis particularly in the early startup of 1994.

- The evidence suggests that Drs. Blanchard and Bishop were slow to respond effectively to concerns that were raised by program staff in the spring of 1994.

- The evidence suggests that Drs. Blanchard, Bishop and Craig should have informed their respective vice-presidents in writing and in detail of the anesthetists' decision to withdraw services in May 1994.

- The evidence suggests that the program should not have been allowed to return to full service in September 1994.

- The evidence suggests that Dr. Odim's membership in the panel of surgeons that reviewed each surgical death for the Children's Hospital Standards Committee had the potential for a serious conflict of interest when the death involved one of Dr. Odim's patients.

MONITORING OF ISSUES AND PROBLEMS OUTSIDE OF THE HSC

FINDING:

- The evidence suggests that the Chief Medical Examiner's Office failed to identify the problems within the Pediatric Cardiac Surgical Program in a timely fashion.

- The office of the CME did not track the deaths by program. As a result, they were unable to identify trends in the PCS program. The office of the CME was not informed of the changes of the program, particularly withdrawal of the anesthetists' services in May. Since these events were linked to concerns about mortality, they should have been communicated to the OCME.

Delays in autopsy reports also contributed to the lack of information received by the OCME.

RECOMMENDATION:
It is recommended that the Office of the Chief Medical Examiner develop a protocol requiring hospitals to inform that Office of significant changes in the delivery of medical services.

It is recommended that the OCME maintain a database of hospital deaths.

It is recommended that as part of their investigation into the patient's deaths the CME's investigators (MEIs) conduct preliminary interviews of nursing and medical staff who had been involved in the patient's care.

It is recommended that for CME cases the Chief Medical Examiner arrange to have autopsies performed by pathologists not affiliated with the hospital where the operation has been performed unless it is unreasonable or impossible to do so due to distance, time or expertise.

It is recommended that the OCME develop guidelines for pathologists to follow in obtaining information before performing an autopsy in CME cases. These guidelines should not place over-reliance on anyone whose involvement might have contributed to the death of the patient.

It is recommended that the OCME establish reasonable timelines to complete autopsies, prepare and forward preliminary results and complete the final reports, including the completion of necessary laboratory work.

It is recommended that the CME insist on compliance with reasonable timelines for the preparation and delivery of autopsy reports.

It is recommended that the HSC and other hospitals amend their autopsy consent forms. It should be made clear that hospital might wish to retain organs and other specimens from the body of the deceased patients. Families should have the option of withholding such consent, while still consenting to the autopsy itself.

HUMAN AND MEDICAL ERROR

Judge Sinclair wrote at length about human and medical error in his report. Briefly, judges adjudicating inquests must consider the factors involving human and medical errors occurring within the hospital and determine if changes are needed to prevent them from happening again. Human beings make mistakes. It is impossible to design a perfect system where no one will make errors but there must be mechanisms to correct them if they occur.

Error can be handled in two ways. Blaming or learning from it. They are unplanned events which can or do result in negative consequences. Errors coupled with a patient's medical condition can result in a critical incident.

In 1994, there was a clear lack of a timely and critical examination in the hospital of the events that occurred in the operating room. M&M rounds, which were supposed to be a mechanism where mistakes could be identified and discussed, failed. The Wiseman Committee was intended to provide a process as well. It failed.

The Pediatric Death Review Committee of the College of the Physicians and Surgeons that assessed the deaths of these twelve children failed: it did not take place until long after the events in question, it did not interview any of the participants, and did not discuss the "near misses" and mistakes that did not result in the death of a patient.

The Williams and Roy review in 1995 did not attempt to look at each of the cases. It was intended as an overall assessment of the program.

In the end, there was no process at the HSC that allowed team members to comfortably and collectively assess and evaluate the events that occurred in the operating room in a manner that contributed to improvements.

A NEW APPROACH TO THE HANDLING OF MEDICAL ERROR AT THE HSC

"Error is a human reality."

Judge Sinclair recommended the development of a Critical Incident Review Policy. It should provide immediate, multidisciplinary identification, management and review of critical incidents and accidents. To avoid impeding communication and facilitate fact finding, the policy should be implemented non-judgmentally. Within forty-eight hours there should be a meeting of a review committee, with either a department head or risk manager chairing the meeting. All those who were involved should be present. The responsibility for ensuring any recommendations coming from the review should be the responsibility of the hospital or regional health authority or equivalent.

A Critical Incident Review should consist of:
- A survey on the scene

- A review of all documentation

- The establishment of a timeline of events

- A review of all other pertinent information

- A review of all pertinent policies and guidelines

Another issue under that heading was Team Performance.

Judge Sinclair stated that problems in leadership, teamwork, communication and decision-making loomed large in the history of the Pediatric Cardiac Surgery Program. He suggested some initiatives to improve team performance that focused on:

- The necessity for team building through a briefing and orientation process that included all players

- The initiation of pre-operative briefing sessions that focused on the plan for the operation and plans to address any contingencies, should problems arise with the patient, equipment or personnel

- The planning and the use of standard operating procedures

- The development of leadership skills

- The provision for team development or maintenance

- Emphasizing team communication

- Clarity in the decision-making process

- A process of conflict resolution

· Post-operative debriefing sessions (for all operations, regardless of outcomes)

· A stress management component

Under Team Training, Judge Sinclair suggested that an important element of team performance is training that is specifically designed to:

· Decrease or reduce the probability of errors occurring.

· Correct errors before they have an impact.

· Contain or decrease the severity of the consequences of those errors that have been made.

RECOMMENDATION:
It is recommended that the Province of Manitoba consider legislation that requires hospitals throughout Manitoba to establish appropriate quality assurance and risk-management programs.

It is recommended that the HSC, in conjunction with the WRHA, develop a quality assurance and risk management program employing the principles and suggestions contained in the report.

It is recommended that the HSC exclude a doctor who has been involved in a case that is under review by any of the hospital standards committees from participating in the decision-making process relating to such a review.

It is recommended that the HSC Department of Surgery develop an appropriate database for all surgical procedures, but particularly for pediatric cardiac surgical operations. The database should include information such as cross-clamp times, cardiopulmonary bypass times, total circulatory arrest times, amount of blood product used and such other relevant information as would allow for the proper monitoring of surgical trends within a given program or for a particular surgeon,

It is recommended that pediatric cardiac surgical data be collected in a way that makes it possible to compare Winnipeg procedures with those performed in other centres.

It is recommended that the HSC establish a clear policy on how staff is to report concerns regarding risks for patients. This policy must ensure that there would be no personal or professional jeopardy to the person who is making the report. It should be clear to every staff member to whom they are to present such reports.

It is recommended that the HSC administration ensure that all staff members are made aware of their responsibility to use incident reports and fully chart problems with the process of delivery of care and any complications in the outcome of care.

THE FUTURE OF PEDIATRIC CARDIAC SURGERY IN MANITOBA

FINDING:

- The evidence suggests that the Province of Manitoba lacks a sufficient population base to assure the establishment of a high-quality, full-service Pediatric Cardiac Surgery Program

- The evidence suggests that there are real benefits to patients to having a high-quality, limited-service pediatric cardiac surgery program in Manitoba that is integrated into a regional Pediatric Cardiac Surgery Program.

RECOMMENDATION:

It is recommended that the HSC, the WRHA and the Manitoba Department of Health pursue discussions with provinces in Western Canada for the development of a Western or Prairie regional Pediatric Cardiac Surgery Program.

It is recommended that a provincial Pediatric Cardiac Surgery Program be developed at the HSC that is limited to undertaking lower and medium-risk procedures but can undertake more complex procedures in conjunction with a regional pediatric cardiac surgery centre.

It is recommended that the Province of Manitoba develop a financial assistance package for families required to travel out of province for surgical treatment of family members. The package should ensure that family members are in no worse a financial position than if the treatment had been provided in Manitoba.

COMBINING THE ICUs

RECOMMENDATION:

It is recommended that as a part of any planned restart of the Pediatric Cardiac Surgery Program, the post-operative care of pediatric cardiac patients be centralized in a single intensive care unit.

REFERRAL TO THE COLLEGE OF PHYSICIANS AND SURGEONS OF MANITOBA

FINDING:

· The evidence suggests that there may be a need for the College of Physicians and Surgeons of Manitoba to investigate the evidence set forth in these proceedings to determine if other proceedings may be necessary.

RECOMMENDATION:

It is recommended the College of Physicians and Surgeons of Manitoba revamp its policies and procedures so that in the future investigations and disciplinary proceedings no longer depend on whether or not a formal complaint has been filed with the College.

It is recommended that the College of Physicians and Surgeons review this report to determine if there are grounds of undertaking disciplinary proceeding against any of the medical professionals involved in the care of any of the twelve children whose deaths were the subject of these proceedings.

INDEX